Wilhelm Haller

The Dark Fire

God's Destructive and Loving Power in Man

With a foreword by Eugen Drewermann

The Dark Fire
God's Destructive and Loving Power in Man

Texianer Verlag
Johannesstrasse 12, D-78 609 Tuningen,
Deutschland
www.texianer.com

ISBN: 978-3-949 197-66-6

Translated from the German by
© 2021 Stephen A. Engelking

German Edition: Das dunkle Feuer
Gottes zerstörende und liebende Kraft im
Menschen
© 1994 Wilhelm Haller
Texianer Verlag 2021
ISBN: 978-3-949 197-51-2

*for
the Dark Ones,
the marginalized,
the failed,
the losers,
the failures,
the unnamed,
the forgotten
and especially for Hennesli*

Contents

Foreword..7

A Justification.......................................11

The Incarnation....................................29

The Emergent..61

The Dark Side.......................................79

The Elemental Force............................97

The Nativity..117

The Unification of Opposites............131

Foreword

A book, like this one by Wilhelm Haller, has an effect of its own. Erich Maria Remarque once said that with the last sentence of a book, an author should have spoken his last word on the subject he has chosen—after that, the critics should write what they want. I think this is the best suggestion I would also make about Wilhelm Haller's book. After all, one only diminishes an author's achievement if one dresses it up in a clerical robe from the very beginning. Nevertheless, it is important to know who the author actually is.

For decades, Wilhelm Haller has been committed to combating the social frigidity of an economic system that is oriented primarily to the principle of "competition" and the goals of "profit" and "interest". For many years he was the managing director of a computer company, from which he left to "do new things from scratch". His religiosity has its "basis in life". Thus, he is one of the initiators of the "Life Houses" (Lebenshäuser) in which many different forms of communitarian shared living are practiced to counteract the disintegration of our society. The core groups of these life houses consist of at least two families, around which a larger number of people are grouped who do not want to or cannot live alone.

There is a weighty reason why a renewal of religious consciousness is called for in our days: This is the factual ambiguity of all religious terms in the shadow of 2000 years of church proclamation. All words from biblical inheritance have meanwhile been rendered empty or their content has been misplaced by the language of church dogma. A few examples suffice to show this: Speaking of "sin" and "original sin" has; far from the original religious problem of a life in radical exposure and despair, degenerated into a topic of moralizing reproaches for petty bourgeois everyday life. Such an important term of Christian "proclamation" as the word "grace" has taken on something so condescending, grave, and domineering in church language that it humbles rather than elevates people. The language of theologians has lost the sensitivity to distinguish, in speaking of God, between actuality and alienation, between self-discovery and external direction, between ego-development and neurosis. The author of the book does not speak the language of the school theologians, is not a scribe of the old school. He speaks of his experiences and the "personal" knowledge gained from them that lead to a deeper reflection.

Eugen Drewermann

A Justification

Actually I had thought that my search and my questioning, concerning the internal and the external, my examination with and around God and the world had been concluded with my last book[1]. Far from it. As the chapter "The Darkness" in particular makes clear, these questions have again been forced upon me from within, forcing me to come to terms with them. This book is the outcome.

I have included the last two chapters of the preceding book with changes and extensions in the beginning of this book. They represent the prelude to my inner confrontation, the first being more a justification of my approach than a statement of content. It is above all a plea to express one's own subjective experiences and convictions, but not to claim that they are universally valid. Above all, I want to make it clear that it is about trying to make sense of internal and external experiences—or even more concretely: subjective impressions of them —and their evaluation from the point of view of my person, that is, from the point of view of

[1] "Neither Sword nor Scepter", Texianer Verlag, 2020.

the human being. This is actually self-evident, because of course no human being can speak of the nature of God himself or even describe it, just as little as an ant would be able to tell comprehensively about the European continent. Man can only speak about God from His own images and experiences.

My central question is whether and to what extent we subordinate ourselves to the law of convention, i.e. also to the church teachings and the general Christian self-image. Whether consciously or unconsciously, this means conforming to the existing "morphic fields", to use a term used by Rupert Sheldrake[2], or to what extent we claim the freedom to "think and also to go our own, novel ways". To walk ones own paths means, of course, groping, stumbling attempts to win new land—painful, slow, laborious, and not without mistakes. The same applies to its description. It remains a stammering, which rather disturbs than clarifies. It is incomplete, cursory and erratic, neither straightforwardly convincing nor scientifically validated. Moreover, this is an account of personal involvement through an inner development that is not completed, but rather one that is taking place. The goal and end of this

---

2   For details see Rupert Sheldrake, "The Memory of Nature".

development can neither be discerned nor foreseen at the beginning of this essay. Hence the disjointed and fragmentary nature that is only meaningful to those who are faced with similar questions and experiences and who experience and express intrinsic and extrinsic reality in a comparable world of images and concepts. This is an essential restriction: I am a man of the end of the 20th century and come from the Judeo-Christian cultural milieu. My narration is influenced by these sources. Thus confined, I will attempt to express that which concerns me.

To begin with, I have to go rather far out on a limb and start with "Old Testament" Judaism because, even as a Christian, I am not spared the observation that the search for fresh sources inevitably leads me beyond Christianity to Judaism. It is precisely in dealing with the real concern of this book, namely the Dark Side of God, that Jewish traditions, unlike most Christian ones, have faced up to the problem and have not suppressed or separated it. The statement in the Gospel of John: "Salvation comes from the Jews"[3] seems to be confirmed once more. It is all the more surprising that this statement is found there, of all places, since the

---

3   John 4:22

Gospel of John is not exactly brimming with friendliness towards the Jews.

One of the most common prejudices about Judaism lies in the view that its character is determined primarily by the demand for submission to strict biblical laws. This opinion is promoted in Christianity by the predominance of Pauline thought. As is well known, Paul had advocated deliverance from the law through faith in Christ[4]. He therefore became involved in considerable controversy with the Jewish Christian community in Jerusalem. In fact, this Pauline line not infrequently becomes the starting point for a conviction according to which Jesus' disagreements with the leading classes of the land stem from diametrical opposites in which Jesus stands for freedom from the law and the others for submission to the law. This conviction is untenable based on the traditions. For all the generosity Jesus showed in keeping the law, his statement remained unambiguous, according to which even the last iota of the law had to be fulfilled if the kingdom of God was to become a reality on earth.[5]

The concrete historical situation makes the error about Judaism very clear. Whereas in Christianity it quickly developed into the

---

4 Especially in the Epistle to the Romans
5 Matth. 5:17

dogmatization of certain principles of faith—the attempted enforcement or combating of which not infrequently led to murder and manslaughter, the extermination of minorities, and even to long-lasting religious wars—in Judaism the insight prevailed very early on that there were just as many interpretations of the Torah as there were Jews. In the famous disputes between learned Jews and Christians in the Middle Ages this became apparent again and again. Even then, the Jewish side showed much more intellectual agility and individual freedom in all these questions than the opposite side. Here seems to me to be an essential error of some Christian authors who are able to recognize this openness and individuality only in Jesus, but not in Judaism in general.

This widespread misunderstanding can already be seen in the fact that the Hebrew alphabet originally did not have any vowels. Vowels were considered to be the breath of God, which eludes human fixation. Thus, the Hebrew orthography already allowed for an almost unlimited number of possible interpretations, rather than a generally valid dogmatic statement. So it is conceded that every interpretation is ultimately subjective, time-bound, influenced by the spirit of the times and thus changeable. Consequently, this also applies to the respective image of God. Latin, on the other hand, is very precise both as a language and as a script. It is therefore not surprising that Latin became not only the language of Christian dogma, but also of the precise natural sciences. It makes no decisive difference whether the pope and the Vatican are ultimately the decisive authority, as in Catholicism, or whether the Bible plays this role, as is usually the case in the Protestant churches.

In fact, the differences just described also by the above-mentioned authors are not a fundamental problem of the Jewish people, its religion and its language. On the one hand, they are general, recurrent intra-Jewish rabbinical conflicts about the interpretation of the laws—for example, which actions are permissible on the Sabbath—and, on the other hand, they are the age-old conflict, inherent in all religious communities, between priest and prophet, law and freedom, between dogma and change born of the spirit and the immediate, overwhelming experience of God.

This conflict is not only found within Judaism, but equally within Christianity as well as in other religions and religion-like ideologies. In communism, for example, the writings and speeches of Marx and Lenin were and are elevated to quasi-divine revelations and dogmatized.

A Justification

People, and especially the power elites, always tend to codify the traditions and statements of extraordinary personalities into generally binding dogmas with the force of law, enforcing compliance with them. In this context, the willingness to submit to charismatic leaders and the rules they establish seems to virtually encourage the temptation of such personalities to arrogate to themselves divine power and corresponding rights to issue directives. And if they themselves do not succumb to the temptation, as was obviously the case with Jesus, for example, then conflict-shy and dialogue-hostile followers ensure, if only for the sake of their own benefit and convenience, that the dogmatization and the mostly associated exclusive administration of truth and salvation by themselves are not called into question by others. This is classical conservatism, which can be found among orthodox Jews as well as in the Vatican, among evangelicals, pietists and communists, and of course also among other religious or generally ideological groups.

Of course, this conservatism is not fundamentally reprehensible. After all, every community, from the religious congregation to state society, needs an internal order that also regulates the way people live together. Therefore it is not surprising that Paul, after his abolition of the Jewish system of order, recommended his followers to submit to the state order of Roman law[6]. Order must be, but it may not go so far that religious and interhuman experiences from times long past and their interpretation by some privileged people become dogmas and laws in perpetuity. Rather, it is a matter of including the traditions in a dialogue of the living and thus making them the basis and source of the further development of the order, the eternal search for justice and for truth. In this way, space is created for the rectification and improvement of misconceptions and errors, both of previous generations and of one's own. Thus it is admitted that the absolute, the objective truth is accessible to man at best fragmentarily, but his subjective truths on the way of liberation constantly need common reconsideration, rectification and improvement. In doing so, wonder and respect for the great traditions should not be neglected. After all, they are imbued with the dreams and hopes, the longing and suffering of many generations. This gives them content and meaning that not infrequently reach the quality of the sacred and whose concerns we cannot escape.

---

6   This also becomes particularly evident in the Letter to the Romans.

A Justification

It is unmistakable that the individual interpretation of law and justice is given much less space in the Roman thinking of power—with its attempted fixation on eternity—than it corresponds to the Jewish or even the Germanic feeling. In order to recognize this, it is sufficient to compare the Roman imperialist legal systems from the Corpus Juris Civilis via the Napoleonic Code up to our present time and the attempted absolutization of, for example, the Basic Law in Germany, with the jurisprudence of the rabbis, based on the various interpretations of the Torah, or that of the Anglo-Saxon way of thinking with Common Law.

The restriction of all human testimonies to the time-bound, fragmentary and subjective applies naturally also to this book. It does not exclude the fact that I represent my opinion very emphatically and defend it passionately. Quite on the contrary. But I am perceptive enough to understand that my insights are, at least in places, very subjective and will continue to require dialogical discussion in order to provide useful building blocks for the path to the future.

Even if many of the experiences to be included in this process are timeless, it must be recognized that this is mostly true only for the content, but not for the form. That is, even if we grant timeless divine dimensions to the content of such an experience, we must always ask what form this content must take in order to be experienced and comprehended in the here and now. The form may have to be changed, even if the content remains the same. Of course, it must not be overlooked that the content influences the form and vice versa.

In the so-called Ten Commandments, the problem and the most widespread misunderstanding are most clearly recognizable. In the traditions, a preface in which God identifies Himself as the Deliverer and Redeemer[7] is followed in the German-language editions of the Bible by a whole series of "Thou shalt..." and "Thou shalt not..." They are commonly understood as requirements of the law. In fact, the whole story means that when man sets out on the path of liberation from his dependances through God, he becomes free from everything deadly and no longer does it because he no longer has to compulsively act that way. As Ernst Lange, who called the Ten Commandments the Ten Freedoms, had already understood, it is rather about ten liberations than about the compulsive law of ten command-

---

[7] "I
am your God;
Who brought thee out of the land of Egypt,
out of the house of servitude"
(according to Martin Buber)

ments. That is why Martin Buber does not speak of the law, but of God's instruction. This applies equally to the Jew and to the Christian (and to everyone else). So the focus is always on the search for God, as Jesus' parable of the treasure in the field and the particularly beautiful pearl makes clear[8]. The focus is not on the constraints of the law, even if, of course, one presupposes the other, just as in this parable it takes the renunciation of everything superfluous to reach the great goal.

How to find and walk the path to such liberation from dependences and inner constraints is a completely different question. The Jewish proverb "In memory lies the secret of salvation" shows where the path for the answer to this question is to be found.

This quest requires an engagement with collective history and its teachings and traditions as well as with its individual component, that which has shaped us personally. This also includes the willingness to engage with one's own feelings, especially the repressed ones. Here, too, it is a question of an internal and an external, of a departure that aims at a change, a conversion in the innermost as well as in the outermost, just as every therapy for the desired

---

[8] Matth. 13:44 ff.

inner change also almost always requires a change in lifestyle and life circumstances.

For too long and too often, Christianity has pretended and continues to postulate that the Sinai experience, that is, the God experience of meaning, destiny and fulfillment, takes place directly at or even in the flesh and lard pots of Egypt, that is, in prosperity and enslavement as the price often paid for prosperity. The talk of "cheap" grace has done much harm. It is simply a lie. Sinai and Egypt are mutually exclusive, even if, of course, in the sense described, the Sinai experience does not become possible without the Egypt encounter, but presupposes it.

Whoever becomes aware that he lives—figuratively speaking—in the slavery of Egypt, and whoever suffers from it, will have to set out, time and time again. Sinai is outside, in front of us, beyond the desert, but it is always worth the effort, because the path, as the story tells, is accompanied by God. Even if this God is not always a God of proximity, but also a God of distance, not only a God of light, but also of darkness. My experience, which has essentially led to this book, shows that our second great failing is to lie all too often that in darkness lies salvation, that for the process of transformation of the seed into fruit—to use an image of Jesus—the darkness of the earth and its apparent annihilation are decisive. Obviously, salvation grows above all out of sorrowful experience with oneself and with the environment.

It is not, however, about a path of asceticism and self-flagellation, painting our faces with bitterness and sullenness. It is about a path of liberation that can lead man from a four-legged crawling critter of internal and external dependences to the "glorious freedom of the children of God"[9] and make him an upright human being.[10] This path leads through the desert, down into hell, into the cavern, into the dark womb of mother earth, in which the grain of wheat dies and out of that alone is able to bear fruit.

Probably even more terrible in its concrete effects is the increasingly clear insight that Christianity and thus the thinking and actions of Western man are dualistic at their core and that the deepest roots of our aberrations can be found here, from the Crusades to the witch burnings through to Auschwitz. This dualism must have been the mindset shaping the Eastern

---

9 Paul according to Romans 8:21
10 See also Genesis/Leviticus 25:13:
   "I am your God,
   who brought you out of the land of Egypt
   out of your servile estate,
   I broke the bars of your yoke.
   and made you walk upright."

Mediterranean even at the time of early Christianity. Not in Jesus himself, who repeatedly emphasized the "coexistence of opposites," for example, in his statements about how to deal with evil. The love of enemies that Jesus speaks of has the same root. Dealing with the external "enemy" depends essentially on how the internal "enemy" is dealt with. I will only be able to love the external "enemy" when I have lovingly accepted the internal "enemy".

This seems to have been different for the evangelists than for Jesus himself. A comparison of the two temptation stories of Abraham and Jesus demonstrates this. In Abraham's case, it is clearly God himself who instructs Abraham and wants to tempt him to sacrifice his son, i.e. to act according to the general state of consciousness. In the case of Jesus, Satan appears in the temptation story and wants to persuade him to become a messianic personality as is generally expected, namely a promising power politician and a magician. Satan is indeed one of the sons of God in Jewish tradition—especially clear in Job. Common Christianity, however, has in fact made him into a counter-god to be fought, as the temptation story of Jesus according to the Gospels also makes clear.

In contrast to this is the ancient tradition of Judaism, which in spite of all terrible experiences holds on to the monotheistic concept of God and traces not only the bright but also the dark experiences of man in their root back to God himself.

The aberration of Christianity only became clear to me in a lecture by Ilse Schütz-Buenaventura, a Colombian woman, who traces the roots of our almost self-destructive treatment of man and nature back to our dualistic worldview that is hostile to the body and nature.

She says: "Modern civilization, however, which began to develop in Central Europe five hundred years ago, differs fundamentally from antiquity and the Middle Ages in that it arrives at the formulation of the totally invisible as a new principle of power and action against nature and man as living entities. To behave according to the principle of the modern subject as something intangible means not only the assertion of the subject's self in open opposition to living things in general... Modernity... makes nature into its enemy, it is degraded to evil in general, and the realm of abstractions exalts itself above the real."[11]

Elsewhere she underlines this, saying,

---

11 Unpublished manuscript of a lecture given on February 7, 1994, on "Causes of War and the Western Lifestyle from the Perspective of the So-Called Third World."

"Whereas any pre-modern dualism actually still involves a coexistence of two mostly visibly presented instances, modern radical dualism becomes the principally given discord between spiritualized reason as a new level and the material world as mindlessness that must be transformed."

The consequence of this, according to Ilse Schütz-Buenaventura, "could be called a... war against the essential life within us and our natural and social environment".

The immaterial self is understood by us as the desirable good combined with a claim to eternity and is in a constant struggle against our own decrepit physicality. This represents for us the darkness that is suppressed, repressed and fought against as evil. Modern Western man wants to be the master of himself and tries to make all materiality a controlled object, his own as well as that of others. After all, we think we have mastered matter. In the end, however, we have to realize with horror that we are dominated by it for this very reason. Although it seems that theoretical-dialectical materialism has been overcome in the East, practical materialism is growing and flourishing everywhere, in the West as well as in the East. It is a fruit of this way of thinking and is equally evident in our sciences, in our treatment of nature,

A Justification

and in our mode of production and consumer behavior.

From my inner experiences and my thoughts about them, they suddenly became not only a subjective, individual speculation that is ultimately of secondary importance, but a challenge to our individual and societal thinking and actions of the highest brisance. I do not wish to claim that my conclusions are absolutely correct and generally valid. However, I think that no responsible thinking and acting person should evade the question I am posing.

Wilhelm Haller

The Incarnation

It does not need too much sensibility to perceive the world as filled and driven by mysterious forces. Only the darkening of the spirit by the theoretical and practical materialism of recent history has caused this insight to atrophy in many minds. In former times it was self-evident. Nevertheless, even today, every human being suspects, just like his ancestors, that with what our senses perceive and that which can be measured and counted, our world and all happenings cannot be adequately explained. Therefore, it is not surprising that from the earliest times, man has perceived the world as populated with gods, demons and many kinds of spiritual beings. The perceptions in his internal and external world did not allow any other conclusions. He felt more or less helplessly at the mercy of too many forces.

Yet modern man, who distances himself from the ideas of his ancestors and feels exalted above them, ultimately finds himself in a similar situation. However, his idols and demons bear contemporary names and mean concretely that the person concerned bows to the spirit of the times. He submits to some scientific or pseudo-scientific postulates, is driven by addictive desires, such as for fame, career, fortune, and intoxicating, ecstatic states, or seeks to escape his fears by chasing military and economic or other forms of external security. The addictions have remained the same, only the names and terms have changed.

Since the time when the light of consciousness gradually dawned upon them out of the darkness of their animal-like unconsciousness, people have always been occupied with the question of the sources of these driving forces. This applies, like everything that will be said here on this subject, both collectively for the history of the spiritual development of mankind and individually for the path of the individual human being.

Polytheism was and is at the beginning of this path. The multiplicity of the invisible, but perceptible forces leads inevitably to this conception. It took a long time until man developed the courage and the spiritual foresight to trace back the multiplicity of these phenomena to one single source and to push through to monotheism, the idea of one single God. The beginnings of this in Western culture are to be found in the Israelite tradition. They are recorded and are accessible to everyone in the Hebrew Bible, the so-called Old Testament.

This step is for me one of the greatest spiritual achievements of mankind. It is of such boldness that even today only very few are able to comprehend it in a more profound and binding way than just lip service. Indeed, belief in the one God has dramatic consequences in two respects:

One is the first commandment of the Bible, which takes monotheism to the extreme by claiming exclusivity. In the second book of Moses (Exodus), the second verse reads: "I am the Lord your God! I have freed you from slavery in Egypt. There are no other gods for you besides me." The claim to exclusivity, which at first seems downright presumptuous, is derived and justified in a positive sense by the liberating experience of God. This idea also seems to have influenced Jesus, as can be concluded from his parables of the treasure in the field and of the particularly precious pearl, for which the discoverer gives up everything. Ken Wilber is of the same opinion when he deals with our "idols" and writes about them, "Mankind will never, but never, give up this type of murderous aggression, war, oppression and repression, attachment and exploitation, until men and women give up that property called personality. Until, that is, they awaken to the trans-personal."[12]

---

12 Up From Eden: A Transpersonal View of Human Evolution, 1981, p. 286.

According to these testimonies, ultimately only the experience of God, the awakening to transcendence, is able to liberate from enslavement to idols and dependencies.

The other thing that monotheism is about is of an almost shocking nature. It is so shocking that it is mostly hushed up in the churches, although it is also manifested with frightening clarity in the Greek Bible, the so-called New Testament, and especially in the last book of Revelation.

If, as our faith teaches, the one God created everything out of His omnipotence and if, as Jesus says, not a sparrow falls to the earth without God allowing it, then of course He is also responsible for His creation, for the beautiful as well as for the terrible, for the good as well as for the evil. If we declare God to be the God of love and exempt him from the responsibility for what we call evil, this is only possible with common superficial church Christianity if, in a dualistic way of thinking, it gives space in its world of imagination to an equal-ranking opponent of God as the Lord of Darkness. In this context, the equality of rank is decisive. As soon as we grant God a superiority over His adversary, we tie him back into the responsibility for the work of His adversary, at least as long as we consider God to be omnipotent. He could, after all, cripple him or chain him up like a yard dog. There seems to be no way out of this dilemma.

Monotheism cannot release an omnipotent God from the responsibility for everything that happens in the whole creation. Deviations from it lead to a dualism with a God of light and a God of darkness, a Manichaeism, which—admittedly or not—decisively shapes everyday Christianity until the present day.

In order to do justice to the traditions of the Hebrew Bible, this alternative can and must be differentiated, as I understand it. In doing so, we will hold on to God's responsibility for all that happens in and to creation and all creatures, including man. All pain and suffering that takes place without human intervention or fault remains God's responsibility and can only be reconciled with a benevolent, loving God if it is acknowledged that the framework of human insight is limited and the standards derived from it are not so universally valid as to be capable of judgment even in such fundamental questions.

In the sphere of influence and activity of man, he has the freedom to act responsibly and to decide for good or evil. It is this freedom which distinguishes man from the animal. However, it is only those who are no longer unconsciously driven hither and thither, but have become aware of themselves and have matured to this freedom.

In the history of life on our earth it is recognizable that evolution is accompanied at first by a growing physical mobility, which ultimately leads in man also to a spiritual mobility, namely freedom par excellence. However, this does not abolish the laws of nature and the will of God as a principle of order and design. Yet the growing freedom of man presupposes the complementary growing powerlessness of God. The omnipotence of God often mentioned in the Bible and in Christian songs thus proves in our view to be a polarity of omnipotence and powerlessness, which leads to suffering and harm in the case of the aberrations of man, but allows for erroneous actions.

The key term here is "allows". It also appears with Jesus in the well-known image of the sparrow that does not fall from the sky if God does not allow it. Therefore Helmut Gollwitzer is wrong when he says, "So he (Jesus) went the way of the cross, not thinking for a moment that this would be done to him only by the evil world, by the Jews, by his haters, but in the constant knowledge that they all can do nothing if God does not do it to me..."[13] "Do it" instead of "allow" is a dramatic change. Man countenances, God permits. Man is more than

---

13 Quoted from Helga Sorge, Wer lieben will muss leiden (Who wants to love must suffer).

The Incarnation

just an instrument of God. He is at least a henchman with the (perhaps limited) freedom of his own will.

The consequences of Gollwitzer's way of thinking are not only based on a highly problematic image of God. They would be downright horrible for the evaluation of history. For if God had not only "done" the crucifixion to Jesus, then he would also have "done" the Holocaust to the Jews and all the other victims of Nazism.

But let us return to the original Jewish image of God, the monotheism that does not give up the belief in one God despite all the terrible consequences. This belief has shaped the Hebrew Bible, and the consequences are also expressed clearly enough.

In Isaiah in the 45th chapter, God speaks:
> *It is I and no one else:*
> *who forms the light*
> *and creates the darkness,*
> *who makes peace and creates evil,*
> *I am the one who does all this.*

Jeremiah delivers the same message when he says to Baruch[14]:
> *Thou saidst: Woe is me, oh,*
> *for HE adds sorrow to my pain,*
> *I sigh myself weary*

---

14 Jer. 45:3 ff.

> *and I do not find rest!*
> *So—say this to him,*
> *thus HE has spoken:*
> *Be it so,*
> *What I have built,*
> *I must tear down,*
> *what I planted,*
> *I must reap,*
> *and the earth is all,*
> *and thou,*
> *thou wouldst desire great things?*
> *Desire it no more!*
> *Yes, be it so,*
> *Evil will I bring*
> *over all flesh,*
> *is HIS course...*

In the same sense Amos relentlessly asks[15]:
> *Or does a disaster happen in the city*
> *and it is not HE who has done it?*

The ancient Israelites did not shy away from putting the reality of their monotheistic experience of God into sincere words. And even in Luther, the command of man in relation to God still begins with the words: "You shall fear and love God..." In a comparable way, many of the old Good Friday songs contain, at least indirectly, a belief in a terrible God. In contrast to

---

15 Amos 3:6

the common idea of the "loving God", they express in the widespread tradition of sacrificial mythology that He can only be "appeased by the sacrificial death and blood of His own Son".

In the Hebrew Bible, the examination of God's two-facedness, His mercy and His fearfulness, reaches its climax in the Book of Job:

After the presentation of Job and his piety and prosperity, the scene changes to the heavenly council, to which the "sons of God" appear, among them also Satan. So here Satan is not (yet) the equal opponent of God, but a son of God, thus hierarchically subordinated to God and, as the story shows, also subject to God's instruction. In any case, he strictly adheres to the restrictions that God imposes on him.

A dialogue between God and Satan now develops in the heavenly council. The pronouncements of God towards Satan and later also towards Job shock us. They throw such an evil light on the nature and character of God that one has to wonder how such a book could find acceptance in the holy scriptures of the Jews and Christians.

At first, God boasts about Job's faithfulness and then gives him into Satan's power without hesitation. He not only destroys his possessions, but also kills his children. Job does not waver.

Satan then escalates his attack with God's express consent and covers Job's body with festering boils. Job does not falter. But after long arguments with his friends, he declares, "Do you not see that God is wronging me.... All His wrath is kindled against me; He sets me against myself as if I were His enemy." But he does not give up hope: "But no, I know that God, my Advocate, lives! ...Now I want to see him with my eyes, I want to see him myself, not a stranger! My heart goes out within me with longing!" Finally, God answers Job in terms of language and content like a half-wit, whereupon Job gives up and submits to the brute force and superiority: "I am too little, Lord! What shall I say? I put my hand upon my mouth! I have spoken more than I should, I will certainly not do it again!" God then starts again: "...Are you seriously going to question my right and blame me, so that you will be right?"

Job's experience has led man into an existential spiritual crisis that at first seems insoluble. This is not only true for the past or only for Judaism. It is also true today and for every human being. In this story, God appears as an unfeeling monster who carelessly hands over His creatures to the arbitrariness of His wayward son (more clearly: to His own Dark Side). And Job painfully experiences God's brutality in his own body, but does not give up hope for another, brighter, friendlier side of God.

We could dismiss this story as a document of a primitive conception of God that has become meaningless today, were it not for the fact that almost everyone at some point in his life would find himself in Job's position and would not have any understanding for the fate that befell him. In such a situation the ancient story becomes alive—red-hot. Then it has to withstand and give an adequate answer. This timeless topicality is certainly the reason why the story has found its place in the Bible and has remained alive until today.

The path from polytheism to monotheism is not only the path of the spiritual development of mankind, but also the path of knowledge of every single human being. At some point, the collective as well as the individual path reaches the point of encounter with the Dark Side of God, a point which becomes inevitable for the individual at the latest when this encounter is experienced as physical and psychological suffering in his very own destiny.

Neither the common polytheism—with its idols of success, career and prosperity or whatever else they may be called—nor the dualism of a superficial Christianity with its division of the world of the gods into a lord of light (reflected in the immaterial, spiritual self) and a lord of darkness (reflected in the material body and the rest of nature) helps in this situation. But even the conviction of those who see in darkness only the absence of light pales in the face of brutal reality. The flight into a more or less enlightened atheism does not help us any more.

In the existential crisis, polytheism vainly takes flight into the ostensible and superficial. The Christian of dualism tries to split reality and to shift the evil and darkness to the external or to destroy it on the way of self-destruction in the internal and also in the external. In doing so, he falls prey to the scapegoat syndrome and looks for some culprit on whom he can unload his bitterness, without thereby being freed from it. The refusal to perceive the dark as one's own inner reality similarly leads astray. This worldview, traditionally widespread among Christians and nowadays, surprisingly, also among the followers of the New Age movement, succumbs to the dualistic temptation to consider the Dark as evil and destructive. Thus, to avert one's gaze from these powers of darkness in the naive expectation that this will eliminate them from the world. But of course this is an illusion. Even Jesus was not spared the need to confront them before beginning his public ministry—indeed, according to the biblical accounts, he even enters into an active dialogue with the devil.

Regardless of what one may think of the demonic, empirical psychology already proves the existence of "autonomous mental contents", as Carl Gustav Jung carefully puts it. It is clear that these "autonomous soul contents" can be both positive, constructive and negative, destructive in nature, although, as we all know, such a division is superficial and in many cases questionable. Refusing to perceive dark psychic or spiritual realities only leads to their repression, causing a one-sided perception, indeed probably also experience them as destructive forces. John the Evangelist provides a clear example of this process. If we compare John's Gospel and Revelation even with the caveat that, according to the theory of a Jewish researcher, they probably derive only in part from the material of a single source (this view is disputed by most experts; but I base myself on the research of the Jewish historian Schonfield, who comes to this conclusion), a frightening dichotomy becomes clear. The Gospel and the Epistles proclaim a message of love, and the Revelation, above all, a bloodthirsty message of annihilation. It seems as if the message of love finally became too much or at least too one-sided for the main source of these traditions, so that possibly the Dark Side of being became the gateway for images and visions of tremendous destructiveness.

It is certain that the suppression of the dark powers and their reduction to relatively easily correctable results of human aberrations does not do justice to reality and is therefore not a path to salvation. It is necessary to stand up to the fact, which Carl Gustav Jung formulated in his memoirs in this way:

"The Christian world is now truly confronted with the principle of evil, namely with open injustice, tyranny, lies, slavery, and compulsion of conscience.... Evil has become determining reality. It can no longer be eliminated by renaming it. We must learn to deal with it, because it wants to live with us. How this should be possible without the greatest harm is not foreseeable for the time being."

This is the situation in which we find ourselves. For us Germans, it reached a horrible climax in the so-called Third Reich, which has not been dealt with to this day, as can be clearly seen from the armaments mania, unemployment, environmental destruction, the plundering and exploitation of the raw material countries and the racism manifested in the discrimination of foreigners.

The Incarnation

How little we have profoundly changed since then is proven. Apart from the mostly violent outbreaks of our brown heritage, the scandal of the end of 1987, which was only marginally perceived by the public, is proof of this. According to a press release, an apology came from the Ministry of Defense. However, there was no talk of disciplinary measures against the author.

This shows how much we are masters of repression. It would be necessary to perceive the dark realities in us, to take them seriously, to make them conscious. As long as we do not have the courage to do so, we are dully, unconsciously, compulsively dominated by them and driven hither and thither. Only the perception (also in the deeper sense of the word) creates the prerequisite for the confrontation with them (in the actual sense of the word) and for becoming aware of them, as this becomes clear in the example of the temptation of Jesus.

The initial situation is particularly clear in Martin Buber's translation of Genesis 4:7:

Before thy door standeth sin, a lurker.
But thou shalt prevail!

If not integrated, sin, that which is separated ("sin" and "to separate" have the same root word in German), that which is split off, manifests itself as a stubborn lurker, i.e. a being that threatens to subjugate us again and again. But how do we manage to "prevail" over it?

Quite obviously, we must consciously engage with it, deal with it, perceive it and integrate it as a part of our personality. If we fail to do this, for example because we want to "prevail", suppress and subjugate, it will gain entrance in another way and "prevail" on us, as "autonomous soul content". This autonomy can only be avoided or overcome by integration.

Where is this loving God in the history of humankind when, as Jesus teaches us, not even a sparrow falls to the earth unless God allows it?

The answer to this question is of existential importance for us, because a conception in which God is a God of love and/or an uncaring monster would be unbearable for man. It is precisely in this problem that the root of many people's atheism seems to lie.

In the hell of the concentration camp, the Jew Elie Wiesel found an answer that sounds strangely familiar to a Christian, yet to many might seem like sacrilege. Elie Wiesel describes a scene in the Birkenau camp:

"When we came back from work one day, we saw three gallows on the roll call square. Line up. The SS was all about us with threatening submachine guns, the usual ceremony. Three shackled death candidates, among them a child with fine-cut features, the angel with the sad eyes.

"This time the camp capo refused to serve as executioner. Three SS men took his place.

The three condemned prisoners climbed onto their chairs together. Three necks were introduced into the nooses at the same time. 'Long live freedom' shouted the two adults. The child remained silent.

"'Where is God, where is He?' someone asked behind me.

"Upon a signal from the camp chief, the chairs toppled over. Absolute silence reigned in the camp. The sun was setting on the horizon.

"'Caps off!' roared the camp chief. His voice sounded hoarse. We cried.

"'Caps on!'

"Then the march past began. The two adults were no longer alive... But the third rope did not hang motionless: the lightweight boy was still alive.

"He hung like that for more than half an hour, fighting his death struggle between living and dying before our eyes. And we had to look him in the face. He was still alive when I walked past him. His tongue was still red, his eyes not yet extinguished.

"Behind me I heard the same man ask, 'Where is God?'

"And I heard a voice within me answer: 'Where is He? There—there He hangs, on the gallows...'"[16]

The incarnation of God, the indwelling of God in man is Elie Wiesel's answer to the question that has become unbearable, "Where is God?"

However, Elie Wiesel only goes halfway in this story. He perceives the indwelling of God in the victim, in the suffering and maltreated human being, and thus still finds a comforting image of God. He is not able to ask the terrible question about the indwelling of God in the murderer, about the role of God in the deeds of the Nazi henchmen.

This question, which is ultimately the central theme of the Book of Job, is addressed in detail and—I would like to say—unsparingly by Carl Gustav Jung in his work of old, "Antwort auf Hiob" (Answer to Job).

He begins by commenting on God's role in this drama, noting that God's behavior, viewed and interpreted from a human standpoint, is simply outrageous. He describes how the ambivalent attitude of God, already visible in older writings of the Bible, is exposed in all its awfulness. The God who expects strictly

---

16 Elie Wiesel, Die Nacht, Gütersloh 1980

moral behavior from mankind, as made clear, for example, by the Ten Commandments, is Himself profoundly amoral, at least in the way He reveals Himself to man and in the way he experiences and perceives his activity.

With the conception of God as it comes to light in the Book of Job, the relationships between man and his God reach an absolute low point within Judaism, because this God no longer has anything comforting and lovable about Him, even if He subsequently makes amends. Man is left to himself in the cosmic drama, and only the hope "I know that my Advocate, my Redeemer lives" remains as a light in the darkness, as the various settings of this statement in church music already make movingly clear.

It requires a huge step in the development of the relationship with God or the way man experiences and interprets this relationship. This step takes place with the concept of God becoming man, for us Christians in Jesus. Carl Gustav Jung writes, "Here the answer to Job is given... Yahweh's intention1 to become man, which resulted from the confrontation with Job, is fulfilled in the life and suffering of Christ."[17]

17 Carl Gustav Jung is, of course, speaking of his own conception of Yahweh's purpose here.

Jesus teaches about the fatherly God of love. As Karl Herbst makes clear[18], this image of God obviously does not go back to something learned, but to the immediate, personal God-experience during the baptism in the Jordan, where Jesus suddenly experiences God as a loving being ("You are my beloved Son").

However, this does not answer the question of the roots of evil and the responsibility for it. Nevertheless, the teaching of Jesus about the fatherly, loving God is, in view of the story of Job and also of the experience of Job, an event of tremendous importance, as world history also teaches. It even begins a new era, even if new time does not yet dawn for mankind, as Franz Alt has expressed it[19], but now becomes a more concrete possibility, just as the future oak tree is present as a potential in the acorn.

With the incarnation of God in Jesus, the process of mutual reconciliation and rapprochement has reached a decisive climax for Christian perception; however, it is far from being completed. It actually is just beginning, because with the image of the outpouring of the Holy Spirit "upon all flesh" the progressive incarnation of God in man par excellence is strongly signaled and accomplished. This statement may seem

---

18 Karl Herbst, Der wirkliche Jesus, Olten 1988.
19 Franz Alt, Jesus, der erste neue Mann, München 1989.

The Incarnation

hard to digest to some good Christians, but Angelus Silesius, for example, to name only one key witness, stated in the 17th century: "If Christ had been born a thousand times in Bethlehem and not in you, you would still be lost." He becomes even clearer and more generally understandable when he says: "Heaven is in you. Stop where you are running, heaven is within you. Seekest thou God elsewhere, thou lackest but for ever and ever." However, for the sake of clarity, it should be added that this statement also applies to hell, not only to heaven.

In Christianity, the incarnation of God is defined as a historical process, as a stage in the evolution of life on this earth. For the Christian, this evolutionary stage takes its starting point in the person of Jesus. In any case, this statement is possible and permissible from the point of view of human perception and experience, which is anchored in the frame of reference of time and space.

In Judaism, however, the answer to Job can also be found, even if it is not based on a single person as in Christianity. The concept of the Shechina, the divinity indwelling in creation, is not far removed in its core from the Christian image. In a supplication of the Hasidim it is said of her:

She is like the palm tree.

She who is slain for your sake.
And considered like sheep at the slaughter.
Strewn out between those who offend her.
Clinging and cleaving to thee.
Burdened with thy yoke.
The only one to unite thee.
Bound in exile.
Scuffed on the cheek.
Surrendered to the smiters.
Suffering thy sorrow.[20]

Martin Buber has her say, "My face is that of the creature."

Friedrich Weinreb writes: "God says: Let me accompany man. I will, if he will get entangled in the development and threatens to lose himself in it, suffer with, and through this I will lead him back. So then the Shechina, the other side, accompanies man and with him the world and the whole creation... In the duality, which belongs to the essence of creation and already begins in heaven, it is the maternal side that takes upon itself the task of accompanying us".[21]

Elsewhere, Weinreb writes regarding the Job experience:

"But in the end I also realized that all the evil happens to him who divides life himself, and

---

20 Adapted from Buber "Between Time and Eternity (Gog and Magog)".
21 From Friedrich Weinreb, Die Rolle Esther.

then proclaims the part which he can survey with his senses to be the whole of life. He is just afraid of the other part, because it eludes his reason, which calculates according to sense perception. And what cannot be explained by the standards of this view, he calls senseless or even evil. But I believe that Satan, by opposing the comfortably unfolding destiny, only draws attention to the presence of the other side."

The inkling, even the perception of the bright side of God never left Job, even in the darkest hours, but twice he says something that sounds like a mockery or an illusion in the face of reality, for which there seems to be no more room in the actual situation. The one sentence that makes this clear is the statement: "I know that my Redeemer lives", and the other, following it: "Now I want to see him with my eyes... My heart is failing within me for longing." Here a unique dichotomy becomes apparent. From his innermost feeling, a different experience of God dawns on Job than the image of God that his perception of external reality gives him. His feeling detaches itself from his thinking.

The incarnation of God expands His role for human understanding. He does not only remain the perpetrator or the person responsible for the deed as in Job, He also becomes a victim as in

Elie Wiesel, and man can breathe a sigh of relief. The mystery of the inner experience can thus only be interpreted as God's participation and sharing in suffering. In the end, the inner experience seems to contradict the outer reality, because God as victim carries us, while God as perpetrator seems to torment us.

But how Jesus could say: "Be ye therefore perfect, even as your heavenly Father is perfect" (Matt. 5), while at the same time, from his own arduous experience, he asks in the Lord's Prayer: "Lead us not into temptation", remains a mystery for the time being, completely independent of how the term "perfect" is interpreted.

Of what does the perfection of God, which is desirable for man, consist, since the dichotomy in our image of God cannot be eliminated? It seems as if it now becomes a problem and a possibility for both God and man. Carl Gustav Jung writes about this:

"All opposition is God's[22], therefore man must burden himself with it, and by doing so, God has taken possession of him with His dichotomy, that is, incarnated Himself. Man is filled with the divine conflict. We rightly associate the idea of

---

22 Again, it must be made clear that Carl Gustav Jung in this extract thus describes his own conception of God and develops His image of God from the inner experience of Western (Christian) man.

suffering with a state in which opposites painfully clash, and we shy away from calling such an experience salvation. Why this should mean salvation is difficult to see unless the very realization of the contradiction, however painful this realization may be at the moment, it carries with it the immediate sensation of salvation. On the one hand, it is deliverance from the agonizing state of dull and helpless unconsciousness, on the other hand it is the realization of the divine dichotomy, which man can partake of, as long as he does not avoid the affliction and does not withdraw from his vulnerability. It is precisely in the most extreme and threatening conflict that the Christian experiences redemption, provided he does not succumb to it, but takes upon himself the burden of being a marked man. In this way, and only in this way, the incarnation of God is realized in him. In principle, in fact, it does not seem to correspond to the intention of God to spare man the conflict and therefore the evil."

Quite the contrary, I would say. Because from the point of view of man, it is neither permissible to absolve God from responsibility for His creation, nor His children, namely us humans, from theirs. Atrocities with a reference to a God who fails to chain us creatures that more often than not resemble rabid dogs. It sounds paradoxical, but it really seems that way: God is responsible for what happens to us, and we are responsible for what happens through us. But just as God and human beings are inseparable, so too is accountability inseparable.

Accordingly, the incarnation of God does not only refer to His Light Side, which for us Christians is represented in Jesus. The Dark Side of God, for many manifested in the devil, also chooses man as its home, and it is crucially important for man to become aware of this fact. Here lies a great mystery that probably cannot be fully fathomed in a human lifetime. And yet, in view of the massive threat to man and nature in our time, we must face the question. Perhaps a feedback on our initial thoughts will help us.

If we take the idea of God's indwelling in His creation seriously, it means that the process of creation is not comparable to our procedures for producing goods, whose shape and properties are indeed shaped by our mind, but which ultimately become completely detached from us in their existence. Not so with God and His creatures, that is, with life itself.It seems as if God has poured himself into His creation during the process of creation, of course without being completely absorbed in it (that would be pantheism restricting divine existence to His creation), but nevertheless so far that the old adage gains validity: "God sleeps in the rock, dreams in the plant, stirs in the animal, and awakens in man"[23]. But this also means that the indwelling—this shedding of God in His creation—takes place rather according to a serving than a ruling principle, a principle which creates growing free spaces for the ascending evolution through the renunciation of power.

The Christian idea of an omnipotent God is therefore incorrect. At any rate, it is not complete. God renounces His omnipotence for the sake of human freedom.

The way of evolution is a way of growing perceptiveness at the price of growing sensitivity to pain at the same time as growing consciousness and growing free spaces. A snail can probably not appreciate the beauty of the world and a Bach cantata. But it probably also does not suffer when its parents die. However, it also does not kill millions of its fellow species in concentration camps and wars.

Man is destined to savor the heights and depths of earthly happiness and earthly suffering at the price of such polarities. His conscience and the pain sensitivity connected with it be-

23 Ibn Arabi

come thereby the signpost for individual and collective spiritual evolution—the way of salvation.

However, unification, the reconciliation of opposites (but not their abolition) in man not only becomes the goal of human development, but also leads to the unification of opposites in God and in our image of God. Or, as the Jewish Hasidim used to say, to the "unification of God with his Shechina", of the upper with the lower, of the feminine with the masculine, of light with dark, of the "bringing forth" with the "brought forth", as Franz Werfel was able to call it without evaluation. Just as Jesus, according to Christian conviction, did a work for the reconciliation of God and mankind, so every insightful person, driven by the Spirit of God, can and must make his contribution to the same work of reconciliation and redemption by consciously "taking up his cross", by integrating the dark, by perceiving it, by taking it seriously. Probably in this responsibility lies the real meaning and dignity of man.

Quite obviously evolution, as already mentioned, progresses on the path of growing consciousness and perceptiveness at the price of growing sensitivity to pain. In any case, at the human level, the evolutionary path seems to be a path of experiencing suffering, where higher consciousness is paid for with greater sensitivity to pain. Gandhi wrote, "Suffering is the law of the human race." We become increasingly capable of experiencing suffering, as well as joy, in all its depth. In this way, the actual transformation into humanity takes place in us and within us.

It appears that the energy from which the thrust along this path is fed comes from the tension between the opposites to which we are subjected, opposites within the personality itself and opposites in relationships with the environment.

Man is placed in these contradictions. It is necessary to perceive this, to accept it, to endure it and to let it become fruitful. That these dichotomies manifest themselves often enough as suffering, therein lies the tragedy and probably also the greatness of man.

Temptation threatens in several respects. We run the risk of repressing the contradictions out of cowardice and aversion to pain, of splitting them off and blaming them on scapegoats or even refusing to perceive them. If we fall prey to this temptation, by whatever means, then the dark pole of opposition takes on a life of its own and leads us to ruin.

However, the integration of our dark sides—individually and collectively—has not only existential psycho- and social-hygienic significance. When viewed from the limited human standpoint, it also serves the salvation of God, helping to overcome the dividedness of God or our image of God by contributing to the unification of God not only, as the Hasidim say, with His Shechinah, but, even more concretely, with His Dark Side as well.

Jesus' example may be representative for many. With his commandment to liberate evil through good, Jesus does not see evil as something diametrically opposed to good, but rather as a preliminary stage, as something that is emerging that carries within it the seed of good. Thus, for Jesus, evil is not something unchangeably static that must be fought and destroyed, or indeed imprisoned and suppressed, in keeping with the dualistic worldview with its scapegoat syndrome. Rather, it is something living, to which the ability to change is inherent as a possibility, without the fundamental polarity being annulled by it.

The Jewish Hasidim speak of the so-called "evil impulse" and compare it to fire, which is able to emanate light and warmth.

All this is for the moment only gray theory, however. It has to be asked what may have prompted Job to claim that he knew that his "Redeemer lives" and why his heart is consumed with the longing for God when, at the same time, he is having such terrible experiences. It is the same question that came to me in my encounters with a young acquaintance who was terminally ill with cancer and in a few months went through the journey from unsuspecting young person to death. At first he was all rebellion and resistance. It is clearly evident that he went through the stages of development described by Kübler-Ross in the last phase of his life. A shattering and moving experience, however, was the last encounter a few days before his death, when he confessed with shining eyes that he had found peace and no longer needed consolation. In other words, a Job who had experienced that "his Redeemer lives," a man who, behind all the superficial but initially overwhelming meaninglessness of his pain, suffering and misery, had experienced a deeper meaning, the other God. Not on the level of thinking rationality, however, because on that level the senselessness cannot be penetrated, but on a level behind or below it, on which all argumentation ceases and makes room for an inner experience that does not abolish suffering, but transforms it.

Empty slogans are no longer valid in such a threshold situation. This is the hour of truth, when the chaff of theories and religious dogmas is separated from the wheat of inner experience. Here it becomes recognizable what is essential in life and what are marginal phenomena. So if we are looking for the golden wheat of the lasting, imperishable, then it is most likely to be found in such boundary situations.

The Emergent

In Exodus, the second book of Moses, we are told how the people of Israel built and worshipped the Golden Calf on Mount Sinai during Moses' absence, and how subsequently the punishment announced by God—namely, the extermination of the entire people—was averted by Moses' objection. It says there in conclusion: "Then the Lord refrained from carrying out his threat and did not destroy his people."

We can dismiss this story, as well as others with a similar meaning, as a document of a primitive conception of God. This view cannot be dismissed out of hand. However, it is not sufficient to resolve the mystery of God described here, Whose actions can be influenced by man. Probably the God conception of the Hebrew Bible holds more than only a breath of the truth of God, when it describes Him with such stories for our human-earthly perceptive faculty as an emerging one.

Bonhoeffer writes:
People go to God in their need,
find Him poor,
reviled,

without shelter or bread,
see Him engulfed by sin,
weakness and death.
Christians stand with God in His sufferings.[24]

God, however, does not seem to be the only suffering one whom Bonhoeffer is describing here. His participation in the fate of his creatures probably goes even further.

It really seems as if God has not only incarnated progressively in the process of creation, but has also gradually limited Himself in His omnipotence on this path, to such an extent that it finally depends on man which traits of God become reality on earth.

The way of creation is quite obviously a path of growing freedom for all creatures. It begins with minerals with an almost complete mechanical solidification, with plants it attains the ability to move, even if they remain essentially bound to their location. In animals, the attachment to location is largely overcome, but behavior and action remain constrained by instinct and controlled by drives. Only man is able to step out of the dullness of the unconscious life of instinct into the freedom of consciousness and the freedom of deliberate action.

---

24 Bonhoeffer, Widerstand und Ergebung, München 1951.

This freedom, of course, extends only as far as God releases man from his omnipotence and control. The idea of an omnipotent God cannot be reconciled with the image of human freedom. And since, as the Bible repeatedly makes clear, God is a liberating God and human freedom is central, this means that God's working power is a serving and not a ruling one. It is therefore no more than an offer that leaves open its acceptance or rejection and also the way it is used, even if only in a more or less wide range of human freedom. It may well be that the divine goals will inevitably be realized on this earth. The how and when, however, seems to be largely open, because these goals manifest themselves as an urge and as a longing and not—mechanically-technically speaking—as a power connection which leaves no room for maneuver and thus no freedom of choice.

Accordingly, man is an autonomous, sovereign, responsible being whose task it is to go his own way, alone and with the help of his fellow men, for good or for evil. He acts on his own responsibility. God gives him the power to do so. He fulfills his destiny and becomes a whole person, however, only when God's desire becomes his own.

However, this does not yet fully grasp the greatness, dignity and significance of the human being. According to the Hebrew Bible's concept of God, man's task and responsibility go even further.

If, as is demonstrated by history, it takes man's objection to prevent God from "making good His threat", then man not only has unrestricted responsibility for his own behavior and deeds, i.e. also for Auschwitz. He is furthermore responsible for the transformation of the indwelling God. This means that the manifestation of God on this earth, as far as a human being is able to describe this in the spatio-temporal limitation imposed on him, develops from the primitive murderous-vengeful to the behavior as Jesus described it—for example, according to the so-called Sermon on the Mount. According to this, man has to go on the way of redemption with the help of the divine powers offered to him for himself, for mankind, for the whole creation—and for the indwelling God Himself. He is therefore an independent instrument for the liberation of the indwelling God from the self-imposed prison of a low level of development.

The story of Jesus' temptation also shows that the dark, the "primitive" indwelling God needs and wants inner resistance, inner conflict. An essential element of this "primitive"

God is described in the life story of Jesus as the devil. But the devil in the Hebrew Bible is not a counter-god of equal rank as in everyday Christianity, but one of the sons of God, as this becomes particularly clear in Job. According to this, the devil is a certain element, a certain side of the one God. In fact, it is only common dualism that makes him a Christian devil, that is, when he is split off and when we try to suppress his existence. In reality, he corresponds to the Dark Side of God and awaits redemption on the path of liberation through man. Jesus teaches to liberate evil through good. This happens when dualism becomes polarity through man as the connecting link.

Carl Gustav Jung calls what becomes recognizable of it in the human psyche, the shadow, and speaks of the necessity of its integration in the sense of this redemption. By this he (only) means the aspect which concerns the salvation of the person concerned, but altogether it is the same process.

Thus, we experience not only the God of light, who meets us above all in silence, an experience that John of the Cross, one of the great mystics, describes with "a gentle, silent glow". In addition, we also experience the dark indwelling God, but mostly in a painful way, which points to a task to be solved. Thus God meets us transcendentally with his timeless love and also immanently as the emerging and transforming one. One side can be described as masculine, the other as feminine and can also be experienced, as Friedrich Weinreb means when he says that the feminine, the maternal side of God, the Shechina, accompanies man into earthly reality.

Obviously, both sides represent different images, impressions and experiences for the individual person, however. It is therefore probably impossible to develop a generally valid representation. Nevertheless, individual, subjective speculation is probably not only permissible, but also helpful and salutary.

It seems as if God's indwelling in His earthly creatures is connected with a restriction to their behavior and ability to act and as if the evolutionary process is also for the indwelling God an ascent from a dawning in the rock to the emerging of consciousness in man up to the heights of His cosmic being with His all-embracing, timeless love. Man's contribution seems indispensable in this evolutionary process. This is probably what the ancient Jews meant when they spoke of the task of man to contribute to the union of God with his Shechina, namely his indwelling reality[25].

---

25 For further reading, see Martin Buber, Zwischen Zeit und Ewigkeit

The indwelling God, who is probably identical not only with the Jewish Shechina, but also with the Great Mother, the Goddess of Nature, corresponds in His "consciousness " to the "consciousness " of the various members of creation and unfolds according to the higher development of man, which He, as it were, accompanies and thus corresponds to their respective state. Through the inherent longing for union, for unity, a fruitful tension arises as a driving force for further development, the path of salvation, the history of salvation.

From depth psychology we know that Yahweh not infrequently reveals himself in dreams as an animal man, and Count Dürckheim reports from his therapeutic work how the split-off and repressed Great Mother eats her children. (That our image of God as the Great Father has caused even more terrible things, as history shows, should only be noted in passing). Here early forms of a development become visible, which make their stages clear.

Organic evolution, which has essentially long since been completed, is followed by spiritual evolution, of which man is the bearer and crystallization point. Symbolically speaking, he has his head in heaven and his feet on earth. He is the connecting link for the energy flow of the divine power between the cosmic and the earthly indwelling God and responsible for the overcoming of dualisms and the restoration of the unity between the eternal, timeless and the earthly-time-bound, a unity which manifests itself earthly-humanly as polarity, namely in above and below, in light and dark, in good and evil. And so the love "from above" meets the longing "from below". Its source is ultimately the same, even if the "from below" has taken on manifold and different forms on its way in creation and not infrequently manifests itself for man as "evil".

Man can thus experience both freedom and security, two of his basic needs, which can be compared to individuation and socialization, in the two aspects of God, the masculine principle of liberation on the one hand and the feminine principle of security on the other. He can experience them in a positive way only through his contribution to their union.

Thus, the limitation of God's omnipotence in the realm of man's earthly reality does not only go so far that God withdraws for the sake of man's freedom, so as not to seriously limit it. It even means that the manifestation of God's infinite love on this earth and its experiential reality is made dependent on man's behavior and actions in a way that makes man in his particular personalities, such as Moses in our story, appear more responsible, more benevolent and more merciful than God Himself—but obviously does not just make him appear, but actually is. The earthly manifestation of these very divine traits actually seems to depend on man's "preparing a place" by his thinking, speaking, behaving and acting. Otherwise it would remain a possibility, but would not become an earthly reality. This is probably what is meant when we talk about preparing the way for the Lord[26].

Three stages emerge on this path, corresponding to the three concepts of spirit, soul and body: divine impulse, human possibilities, earthly reality. Divine impulse, the vision of great harmony, comes from our image of the transcendent God. It is the basis of the divine history of salvation and the driving force of man, but it is only a possibility, a possibility indeed, which will become reality at some point because of its inherent dynamism. But the how and when seems to be very much influenced by man. Man turns this possibility into concrete earthly reality. Thereby the request in the Lord's Prayer, "Thy will be done on earth as it is in heaven," becomes reality in our world.

---

26 For example Is. 40:3

Thereby man fulfills his destiny and thus unites the "God above" and the "God below".

Certainly, on this path of incarnation, aberrations are also possible. They consist above all in arrogating power to oneself and exercising coercion or in objectifying the creative spirit, directing it outwards.

Both sides, in the former case, are in danger of losing their humanity and becoming superhuman and subhuman. Both sides thus lose opportunities for inner growth and spiritual maturity. Indeed, the dialogical interaction between equals is indispensable for such.

The creative spirit in the latter case no longer primarily serves the transformation of man and thus his behavior, but instead technical innovation and other materially based ways of salvation, most of which take on addictive forms and then correspond to the biblical idols.

Every human being is a microcosmic segment of the cosmic drama. His personal abilities and difficulties reflect segments of the great evolution, which fall to each individual as his very own task. Through his maturing process he contributes not only to his personal salvation, but also to the salvation of the world and to the salvation of the indwelling God. This is genuine worship—in the true sense of the word.

Thus, man's freedom is joined by an almost divine dignity and an extraordinarily great responsibility, which really makes him the guardian and steward of the earth both on a small and a large scale. And this extends to his decisive influence on the realization of the divine vision and order among us.

Perhaps the meaning and significance of Jesus' life as the first new man, as Franz Alt calls him, becomes clear for earthly reality in a special way. For him, the ambivalence of the perceivable God becomes apparent in the fact that Jesus says that no one is good except God. And yet he asks in the Lord's Prayer not to be tempted by God. The special significance of this request is made clear by the fact that he does not say it in passing, as it were in an aside, but that, according to tradition, he makes it a daily request in the great prayer and thus a central concern. Thus, he not only trusts God to do it, but also believes that God can be prevented from doing it by man's request. In this way, the divine dichotomy that exists for human perception can be eliminated.

Furthermore, Jesus makes two things clear above all: on the one hand, the overwhelming importance of love and, on the other hand, how man has to face the temptation that can arise from the insights described. The particular theme for Jesus, namely the question of power and violence, not only stands at the beginning of his ministry—namely in the story of temptation—but also becomes the main theme on the last evening and thus acquires bequest-like significance.

Indeed, man runs the risk of succumbing to perhaps the greatest temptation on this path, the delusion of omnipotence, as was seen in particular with the German Nazis, who based their worldview on this point on a probably misunderstood Nietzsche, who famously spoke of the super-human. In the Jesuanic way of thinking, however, the " super-human" is the human being who, although aware of his importance, is also aware of his insignificance in the cosmic drama, consistently renounces power and in all humility tries to make the will of the transcendent God his own out of the love he has experienced, thus contributing to the (re)establishment of unity.

Jesus' special contribution to his own salvation, to the salvation of the world and to the salvation of the indwelling God consisted in drawing from the various traditions and prophetic visions of the Hebrew Bible the strand of love, and, consequently, of non-violence and renunciation of power as the actual divine goals and, in the confrontation with the indwelling God (according to the Greek Bible, with the devil or the tempter), to have struggled for this strand not only to become the earthly guiding principle, but to have "incarnated" itself in him and thus become an earthly reality for the salvation of all.

Christians as yet have only rudimentarily grasped this, as the disputes over questions of armaments and governmental power and the dualism practiced in these matters makes clear time and again. Through his life and teachings, nonetheless, Jesus has made a decisive contribution to overcoming this dualism and transforming it into a polarity, i.e., into an arc of tension that contains both sides, thus allowing them to become fruitful.

The dualism overcome by Jesus, but still dominant among most Christians, sees on the one hand a heavenly God of grace, mercy and love and the validity of the Sermon on the Mount for domestic and private life derived from it, while on the other hand an earthly God "who made iron grow"[27] and of whom it

---

27 Ed: From "Der Vaterlandslied" (Song of the Fatherland) by Ernst Moritz Arndt, 1812:
The God who made the iron grow,
Ne'er wanteth slaves or chattel,
He gave man saber, sword, and spear,
To fight His righteous battle!
He gave to him His heart and breath,
His passion of expression,
So he would fight unto the death,
'Gainst tyrants and oppression.

was said on the soldiers' buckles: "God with us", i.e. a God who also blesses murder and manslaughter. Regrettably, many of us are still subject to this dualism, even though the message of salvation from it is constantly on our lips.

Jesus labored at the risk of his life to overcome this dualism, this division, and to restore unity in polarity, the tension that must be endured. To do this, he had to "connect through" to the infinite love of God experienced in a dramatic way in the baptism in the Jordan to unite the light and dark sides of himself—and of God. It is not without reason that the stories of the baptism in the Jordan and of the temptation in the desert in the traditions represent the prelude to Jesus' public ministry. They reflect the two aspects of God, which are to be united by bringing the dark, the primitive, the indwelling "part" of God, bound to the evolutionary course of time, closer to the timeless-eternal "part" of God, i.e., not subject to evolution, which for earthly-human perception includes the transformation from dualism into polarity.

Does such a change in the common conception of God have a concrete impact on our standing within the world and on our interaction with reality, or does it represent nothing more than theological speculation divorced from reality?

Carl Gustav Jung tells the story of his encounter with the North American Pueblo Indians[28] that could be significant for this: One of the Pueblo chiefs answered his question, "Do you think that what you do in your religion benefits the whole world?" by saying, "After all, we are a people who live on the roof of the world, we are the sons of the Father Sun, and with our religion we help our Father to walk across the sky every day. We do this not only for ourselves, but for the whole world. If we can no longer practice our religion, then in ten years the sun will no longer rise. Then it will be night forever."

Subsequently, Jung initially does address European rationalism, out of which we "smile at Indian naiveté and feel exalted in our cleverness." But he continues and says:

"But the fact that man feels able to respond fully to the overpowering influence of God and to give a substantial recompense even to God is a proud feeling which elevates the human individual to the dignity of a metaphysical factor. 'God and us', this equivalent relationship, probably underlies that enviable serenity. Such a man is, in the fullest sense of the word, in his place."

---

28 A. Jaffé, Erinnerungen, Träume, Gedanken von C. G. Jung, Olten 1971.

An alcoholic, for example, would have to suffer in a similar way when he learns that his confrontation with his addiction resembles the temptation of Jesus in the desert. The tempter, however, on the one hand represents the Dark Side of God and not a split-off devil as a counter-god who virtually challenges the repression. On the other hand—and this seems to be even more important—this dark God needs redemption just as much as the alcoholic himself. Thus, his difficult path serves not only himself—which many have become completely indifferent to in this situation anyway—but also the redemption of the dark indwelling God. What he does or does not do, therefore, reaches beyond his own state of mind. Here, too, man is able to grow "to the dignity of a metaphysical factor," to speak with Jung, and to give his life a new meaning.

This would mean in concrete terms that while man should love his addiction and the God of his addiction as an essential part of his personality, his self-therapy and worship should aim at no longer becoming addicted to it. Again, the parallel with the temptation story of Jesus makes clear what is at stake.

Well, I have melted thee down,
not for silver's sake,

*tested thee in the furnace of misery.
For My sake, for My sake
I will do it.
(Is. 48, 10)*

The Dark Side

"We experience... not only the Light Side of God, which we encounter above all in silence, an experience that John of the Cross, one of the great mystics, describes as a gentle, silent glow. In addition, we also experience the Dark Side of the indwelling God, though mostly in a painful way, which is indicative of a task to be solved."

This is what I wrote in the preceding chapter, which in its outline was written some years ago[29]. But, as I realize and confess in retrospect, I did this without grasping that it concerned and concerns me very personally, that I myself saw and sought God only in the Light, in silence, and not also in the Darkness.

Yes, I wonder how I could even have made such a statement. Once again, I have the impression that the assertion went beyond my understanding at the time and that I only became clearer about the content later. To make this clear, I have to go rather deep and talk about personal inner experience:

---

29 In "Neither Sword nor Scepter", Texianer Verlag, 2020.

Decades ago, I had a vision in which I was standing at the bottom of a staircase, while an animal-like man, resembling a gorilla, was standing at the top, blocking the staircase with his teeth bared. Paralyzed by fear, I remained standing at the bottom. Finally, an inner warmth, even a love for the monster germinated in me, making it smaller and more harmless. The blockade dissolved.

This image rose in my memory again and again in past years, but without seriously touching or occupying me. In the recent past, however, this dream figure seemed to come closer to me as an image of the dark, indwelling God, externally and internally, spatially and emotionally.

When I let myself engage with it, I see and feel a neck that forms a flat hump in the area where it joins the back. I stroke it, see and feel dark fur, not silky, and woolly like a bear, but rather bristly. I ponder for a long time, looking for an experience that would allow a comparison, until after some time, to my great surprise, I remember the blanket of a wild boar at my brother's house. It feels like that. That's it!

This supposition is strengthened by a recent dream in which I hurl a log against a wall (standing on the left) in a kind of rite for an oracle. The plaster comes off, revealing a spiral-shaped stone (a symbol of the womb, I am told), which in turn reveals a boar's head of unbaked gray clay. I do not know what the dream means, essential to me is only that the boar appears again.

It is weird—an animal man with the fur of a wild boar. The book about the black moon taboo comes to my mind,[30] in which there is talk about a wild boar myth, as I remember vaguely[31]. It would have been even nicer if the author, a (former) Württemberg pastor, of whom I have not heard much good in the past, had found an important truth for me. In typical male arrogance, I actually wanted nothing to do with it. But now I have obtained the book and have begun to read it. And it moves me so much that I feel something very important is beginning for me here, even if I don't know where the path will lead me.

Finally, I remembered the story of Rebekah's twins,[32] which first touched me because the conflict between the two had already led to a quarrel in the womb. When the expectant mother inquired, she learned that two nations would come forth from her children, one to

---

30 Jutta Voss, Das Schwarzmond-Tabu, Stuttgart 1991.
31 With this I do not want to claim that my inner image of the wild boar is identical with the wild boar myth described by Jutta Voss.
32 In the Bible Genesis 25.

serve the other after being subjugated by the latter. The one child, Esau, who, according to the legend, was already heading for the pagan temples in his mother's womb, was covered with reddish hair all over his body, as if with fur. And if later the other one, namely Jacob, deceived his blind father Isaac by covering his hand and neck with strips of goatskin so as to pretend that he was Esau, then it should be clear that with the figure of Esau, the image of the animal-like man, also appears here too—the archetype of the animal-man, who is subjugated, suppressed, repressed and is supposed to serve the other, but who out of his suppression instead of serving the other, energetically makes room for his life force, as the story makes clear again and again.

Again, therefore, we have a picture of dualistic division, of secession—two different children, two peoples fighting each other to this day— since Esau is considered the progenitor of the Arab nation, while Jacob is one of the progenitors of the Jews.

However, it should not be forgotten that Isaac loved his firstborn son Esau. Perhaps the experience of his attempted sacrifice by his father Abraham was such a profound experience for him that since then the Dark Side had a different meaning for him than for the others.

According to a Jewish legend, Jacob stands for good and Esau for evil.[33] A rabbinic commentary on this story, however, says that "the Messiah will not come until Esau's tears have dried."[34] He knows, therefore, that the so-called evil cannot be permanently split off, betrayed and suppressed.

Esau is a man, and to my mind was the animal man with whom I have been and am dealing with—also male. But perhaps this is a misconception.

Recently I was in a zoo, visiting my brothers and sisters, the apes, not without sorrow for their fate and for the arduous and painful ascent of spirit and goodness in the evolutionary history of life on earth. Do they represent a stage of earthly development and manifestation of the Dark Side of God?

In my search for an answer to this question, another recent experience comes to mind:

During a trip to the USA, I experienced a few days in the wilderness in Maine together with my son. The foliage glowed in the colors of the Indian summer. The lake, the mountain and the sky—everything was radiantly beauti-

---

33 Joseph Gaer, The Lord of the Old Testament, quoted in Edinger, The Bible and the Psyche, Toronto 1986.
34 Myron B. Gubitz, Amalek, The Eternal Adversary, also quoted from Edinger (in the book cited).

ful. And yet I had a feeling of unease, as I had often had in similar situations, though not with such clarity. I felt as if the wilderness was really savage, even brutal, and that life—here in view of the dreamlike beauty perhaps particularly clearly—"groans and awaits the revelation of the children of God"[35]. I felt a dark, for me rather threatening force, perhaps the life force par excellence. This probably contributed to making the inner image of the animal man described at the beginning of this article come alive in me again. This force seemed to me to lack the element of spirit and goodness.

Although there are examples of animals that practice midwifery or even assisted dying, caring love in the animal kingdom is, as far as I know, generally limited to the more or less long-term care of one's own offspring.

In Martin Buber's works, the Shechina, the indwelling deity, once says: "My face is that of the creature"—that is, the face of all animals and all people, of the depraved as well as of the saints. The Creator, or rather the Creator Goddess, thus dwells in her creatures (in all of them!—in those of the light as well as in those of the dark, in the healthy as well as in the frail), participates in their fate, thus suffering with them and

---

[35] In the Bible in Romans 8:19.

wanting to be redeemed, to be "raised" through them. In this path of redemption, man plays an important role, which is decisive for his maturity and dignity.

As we can see and experience every day, little of "spirit and goodness" is visible and tangible in animals and humans. Have they therefore been abandoned by God? Probably not at all. The indwelling Godhead "lives" on the manifest stage of development and hopes together with the creature, "sighing for the revelation of the children of God".

In my opinion, the Shechina, the feminine side of God, which according to Jewish tradition accompanies man into earthly reality, was related to the image of Mary, the "pure, undefiled, bright one", a typical Christian image. This idea was certainly influenced by the fact that for the Jews, as far as I know, the Shechina has nothing to do with the "evil impulse", the Dark Side of experience. But now I have to ask whether in her femininity she does not rather correspond to the archetypal symbol of the wild boar and thus to the creative life force par excellence.

However, in such an approach there is the danger that in traditionally patriarchal-dualistic division the feminine, the wild, and thus the dark is equated with the evil and the destructive, as has been the case through the past centuries, and not as the fertile bounty, the dark womb of Mother Earth, which in Jesus' parable is the place of transformation of the grain of wheat.

That this can also be different was illustrated to me by the most recent image of my inner experience, which surfaced in me during meditation. The bristly animal man was leaning tenderly against my left side, and I took him lovingly in my arms.

I had no problems with the idea of the dark indwelling (female) God during the visit to the zoo with all the creatures that are not so closely related to us and therefore probably seemed endearing to me. However, the more highly developed they were and the nearer they were to me, the more difficult it became—downright tragic—for me. Reality and possibility seemed to me to be far apart and to express themselves in a longing that seemed more and more painful, a "sighing and waiting" as the Bible describes it, even if it "only" reveals itself in a dull foreboding.

The discrepancy between reality and possibility reaches a tragic climax in human beings. This is perhaps even more true for Christians than for other people, since their history is characterized by murderous wars and the extermination of entire groups of people, by the insanity of armaments and by destructive economic wars, while their religion, such as in the Bible's Sermon on the Mount, knows about entirely different realities. These possibilities are characterized by warm-heartedness and mercy, by renunciation of power and non-violence, by the willingness to serve selflessly instead of ruling egoistically. They are the result of a development in which spirit and goodness are manifested.

This insight, however, which is probably there somewhere, does not prevent us, according to the "law of the jungle", as Mahatma Gandhi calls it, from acting like rabid dogs and doing nothing or hardly anything for the Dark Side of God, the dark life force, not only to incarnate, but also to be liberated and thus to find more and more space for the revelation of the "children of God".

Friedrich Weinreb writes[36] that the word "Adam" in Hebrew means "I am the same", and he then compares the nature and destiny of man with God: "If you are a person with all your tragedy then so is God. You are abandoned? So is He. You are not understood? Neither is He, and how! You are looking for love? And how

---

36 Friedrich Weinreb, Frömmigkeit heute, Weiler 1986.

He seeks it!" Whereby the " He " always means also " She". Weinreb writes namely, "... this Hebrew word of the name 'Lord' is grammatically an exclusively feminine word." And further, "Strikingly, the Hebrew word for 'mercy' can just as well be translated as 'womb,' or 'lap.'" I would add that all the other typically Messianic qualities, such as powerlessness, renunciation of violence, warm-hearted forgiveness, could originally be assigned rather to the feminine-maternal side of man (be he man or woman).

As a perpetrator and victim of development, God suffers from reality just as we humans do. In this sense, the sentence in Job is probably also to be understood: "Why does God give light to the weary and life to the afflicted hearts?"[37] This probably refers to those who suffer from the tension between reality and possibility. In them is manifested not only God's Light Side, but also his dark nature. The resulting painful tension urges the realization of further stages of latent possibility. They are therefore the bearers of the hope (of God and of man) for change, for spiritual progress, even if this should not be realized in a perceptible way in them. Their task is probably already fulfilled if they endure this tension and thus remain bearers of hope like a

---

37 Job 3:20

light in the darkness and a place of readiness in which " latent possibilities" can be realized.

The field of tension between light and dark, above and below, shapes the lives of these people not as something temporary, but as something permanent, as something essential to their personality, as something that changes and transforms in the course of life, yet essentially remaining. The great Austrian philosopher of history Friedrich Heer speaks of "people of tension". There is talk of a terrible and fruitful tension, a polarity that contains both poles as indispensable and does not fall into the temptation of splitting into a dualism, a primitive "here good, there evil" and a dualistic struggle between one side and the other, the ancient Manichean war between light and darkness.

The Dark Side of God, in which the behavior of a lower stage of development is not yet liberated, transformed, takes possession of us. It wants to become manifested through us, the human being, as potential carriers of the "holy" spirit and the divine love, and wants to become incarnate. Man is to become the place for the dwelling of the spirit and goodness, not so that the Dark Side of God and its life force on the low level of its earthly manifestation (especially because its bearer is unconscious of it) by overgrowing the old in a crippled way out of attempted repression (which it currently does when soberly observing the individual and collective reality in this world) and thus blocking development. Rather, it should find an inner home in man in which it can be integrated, accepted, liberated and transformed by him as his own Dark Side—as his shadow as Jung calls it. For the most part, we are unconsciously overwhelmed by it today. We fight against it, or we repress it. Both are in vain. The Greek Bible says: "We do not do the good we would like to do, but rather the evil we abhor."[38]

Incarnation means constraint, restriction to the creature's dispositions and possibilities. This frame cannot be burst apart. A cat remains a cat and a dog a dog, even if with domestic animals it is clearly to be felt that they long to extend the frame of their species-appropriate restriction, for example in their need for attention and tender love.

The Bible rightly says: "He humbled himself, taking on the form of a servant."[1] God becomes man. However, He does not only take on the form of a servant in man, but in all creatures. And the aforementioned "humiliation" always means restriction to the behavior of the creature. In relation to man, this means that he "allows"

---

[38] Romans 7:19

it to be the way of creation chosen by God, that his energy, his power, his spirit is "degraded", even abused to the way in which man thinks and acts, a way that is, however, also fed from divine sources. In a macabre way, the motto of the German Wehrmacht soldiers' buckle corresponds to the truth: "God with us." Subjugated, humiliated, abused—but also so desired. The divine longing, the divine will indeed wants something completely different, but it is fed from the sources of the dark depths. And it is given into the hands of man to bring forth from the depths this quite other thing. Thus the insightful man suffers from the discrepancy between reality and possibility. God likewise suffers.

Even the incarnation, the God becoming man in Jesus, means a limitation to the boundaries of this person: Jesus, a man and not a woman. He was a Jew and not a black or a Chinese. He lived in Palestine and not in India or Latin America, and this about 2000 years ago and not 500 or 5000. Like every realization of ideas, the incarnation is also the renunciation of all other possibilities which are otherwise to be found in the world of ideas.

Jesus was also confronted with the terrible problem of God's self-restraint. As is clear from the Gospels, it was above all, one of the prophetic sentences[39] that troubled him. There it says[40]: "Speak to them so that their hearts may be hardened, their ears closed, and their eyes obscured, so that with their eyes they may not see, with their ears they may not hear, and with their minds they may not know. I do not want them to turn back to me and be healed."

How did he deal with this sentence? How could he still preach repentance when he had to know that it might be in vain, that God might not even want repentance in his time?

Isaiah experiences the shock of God's brutal refusal and must also personally recognize the tragedy of the futility of his efforts. Jesus, on the other hand, in a fundamentally similar situation, feels the hope of a later fruit from his life. Luke makes Jesus' reaction particularly clear.1 Jesus does concede, "They shall see and yet know nothing; they shall hear and yet not understand." But immediately afterward he compares this grim fact to the seed that falls into the earth, the unconscious-dark, seemingly dies, and sometime later (perhaps) bears fruit. He comforts himself and us with the fact that the process of transformation takes time, that it leads through the dark phase of apparent

---

39 Isa. 6:10
40 Translated from the German Christian "Einheitsübersetzung" of the Bible.

demise (that this is therefore unavoidable) and that therein lies our hope. So growth is possible, but not according to *our* schedule and not according to *our* ideas.

Limitation to the potentialities of the creature is a self-chosen prison built of God's stones. It is probably an ever stronger "morphic field", as Rupert Sheldrake calls it. And it is obviously tremendously difficult and filled with painful tension to rise above it, busting the prison to form a new "morphic field".

Hoimar von Ditfurth demonstrates that, as in all other steps, every new development in the evolution of man builds upon the old condition. He writes: "... a new beginning has never been possible for it."[41] Thus the diencephalon developed from the brain stem and the cerebral cortex from the diencephalon, and the younger superimposed the older, but without erasing its mode of action. This is true both of the parts of the brain themselves and of the behavioral patterns associated with them, Sheldrake's "morphic fields." "In contrast to the conditions in paleontology, the *fossils* stuck in the older strata are all still alive... They are fundamentally anachronistic."[42]

41 Hoimar von Ditfurth, Innenansichten eines Artgenossen, München 1993.
42 Ibid.

Out of these sources, presumably, the behavioral pattern, the "morphic field" of the "jungle" still firmly prevails everywhere today. It dominates the internal world just like the external world, the small just like the big. Outside, the restlessness towards chaos prevails, because inwardly restlessness towards chaos prevails. This restlessness reigns inside because it reigns outside. Outside is darkness, as we all perceive, because inside is darkness. So it is necessary that light is born and shines out of the inner darkness, even if the way should be laborious and painful. We take the first step towards this when we perceive and accept this darkness within us. This creates the prerequisite for the birth of light.

The Bible says: "The light shineth in the darkness." For the common Christian far-sightedness, which is dualistic, i.e. Manichaean, this means that the divine light shines in the demonic darkness and that in doing so the darkness must be fought and defeated. In this sense, the crusades of the Middle Ages were justified, as were the wars of more recent times. It was only necessary to demonize the respective opponent, portraying him as a child of darkness. Ronald Reagan, as president of the United States, provided the most recent example of this way of thinking when he referred to the then Soviet Union as the "evil empire" without any subtlety. Nobody is as naive as Reagan nowadays, but the basic attitude he displayed has not changed. We still believe that we can destroy what we call evil by fighting it, on both a small and a large scale, individually and collectively, politically and religiously, as is clearly illustrated by our image of St. George's or St. Michael's fight with the dragon.

Nevertheless, not only is light of God, but also darkness. Or even more concretely: For our human perception, God is not only light, but also darkness- not only light, but also its source, darkness, the starting point of the elemental force, the life force—probably symbolized by the wild boar that Jutta Voss speaks of.

From Jesus we know that it is not a matter of fighting evil, but of liberating it through good. The prerequisite for this is to recognize it as divine and to accept it as such.

The dark indwelling God wants to live and he wants to transform, just as light and warmth want to rise from the dark fire. It is important to know two things. Without the dark, the consuming fire of God (how often, especially in the Hebrew Bible, the fire of God is mentioned!) no light and no warmth can arise. The fire is always the origin. For this it is necessary to prepare in our hearts a place for the union of these apparent opposites.

The Elemental Force

As Jutta Voss impressively points out[43], the way patriarchal and dualistic Christianity deals with the female wild boar is most clearly depicted in the fairy tale of the brave little tailor. There the furious wild boar is locked up in a chapel by the little tailor having pursued him there. The tailor himself crawls through a window and saves himself. In the fairy tale, the wild boar remains locked in the chapel—in the church, that is.

The fact that this scene does not refer to a lifeless story, but rather to something very much alive, becomes clear from the fact that to this day there is still talk in the vernacular German of literally, "letting the sow out" when one wants to go over the top.

For all we know, it is the primordial female force that is being symbolized by the wild boar. Moreover, we know from history that the attempt to deal with this force by the method of the fairy tale is doomed to failure. This is not only proven by the witch burnings of the Middle Ages and the psychological damage that

---

43 Jutta Voss, The Black Moon Taboo, Stuttgart 1991.

celibacy still causes today. It is also proven by the rapes that happen every day in our country, whether individually in our seemingly peaceful society or in large numbers, as is evident from the ghastly reports from the former Yugoslavia.

The dragon seems to play a similarly fatal role as a symbol for the Christian man as the wild boar. It is much older as a pictorial story than the fairy tale of the brave little tailor and appears in many traditions. Surprisingly, it can be seen that the dragon stands for evil in Western sensibilities. Yet in Asia it is quite different.

The dragon plays an essential role for German culture in the Siegfried saga. In comparison with other dragon stories, it is characterized above all by the fact that Siegfried, after defeating the beast, smears himself with dragon's blood and thus becomes invulnerable—except for a spot on his back. His ideal is invulnerability, invincibility. But this remains an illusion, as the rest of the story shows. Siegfried's wife Kriemhild tells Hagen about the "sore spot," and he uses this spot to stab him in the back.

Siegfried sacrifices the sensitivity of his skin for the illusion of invulnerability. His contact surface with the outside world is blunted. He actually becomes an un-human being with the characteristics of the vanquished and the defeated. All in all, it is probably not a story worth emulating.

And yet Siegfried is still a role model for our power elites. In order to manage their tasks according to common values and standards, they try to "not let things get to them", such as not perceiving the fate of the people they influence and only registering it from the safe distance of hierarchical detachment, so-called constraints and benchmarks instead of human faces.

In the most important dragon stories I know, the dragon guards a treasure in an underground space, usually a cave—the hell or the dark womb of Mother Earth? He exercises a regiment of terror over the inhabitants of the area and must be appeased and satisfied by regular human sacrifices (usually virgins). His domination can only be overcome by being defeated in battle by a warlike young man. However, it turns out that for every head cut off, a new one grows back, in some stories even several. In the Greek legend, the Hydra even has seven heads. The dragon is almost impossible to defeat by fighting. But perhaps he should not really be defeated and destroyed? Michael Ende, at least, seems to think so when he lets the dragon thank him "for overcoming me without killing me. Whoever can overcome a dragon without killing him helps him to transform". Michael Ende has his dragon go on to say, " No one who is evil is particularly happy about it, you see. And we dragons are actually only evil enough for someone to come and defeat us. Unfortunately, though, we usually get killed in the process. But when that's not the case,... something very wonderful happens ... "[44]

Thus, here too, the common method of destroying the evil enemy, of murder and manslaughter for the most part, leads to the desired goal in extremely few cases.

There is a third image that suggests to me that Judaism, in the course of its spiritual development, had already found a salutary alternative to the futile "fight against the wild boar or the dragon" thousands of years ago. This is a fight that most people, whether alone or together with others, have been waging more or less unsuccessfully to this day.

The image of Abraham's temptation rose in my mind as I searched for examples of confrontation with the Dark Side, admittedly for most Christians an inadmissible comparison with the wild boar or the dragon.

It is the story of Abraham, who set out to sacrifice his son to God. The person of Abra-

---

[44] Michael Ende, Worte wie Träume, Freiburg 1991.

The Elemental Force

ham is already of great importance because he is considered the common progenitor of the Jewish, Christian and Muslim religions. In addition, Mount Zion, according to tradition the sacrificial site of Abraham, is considered the central sanctuary of both Jews and Muslims. Yet Mount Zion is also a place of greatest holiness for Christianity. So this is a story of extraordinary importance for Western mankind.

What has been handed down is actually rather gruesome. The account is related in essence to the dragon stories: Abraham is ready to sacrifice his only beloved son to God and sets out to perform this terrible ritual. Only at the last moment does an inhibition overcome him, and he refrains from slaughtering his son.

What does the story really want to say?

The Bible says simply[45]: "When Isaac had grown taller, God wanted to put Abraham to the test. 'Abraham,' he cried. 'Yes, I am listening,' Abraham replied. 'Take your son,' God said, 'your only son, the one who is dear to your heart, Isaac! Go with him to the land of Moriah, to a mountain I will name to you, and offer him there to me as a burnt offering.'"

Does God really want this atrocity, or at least the willingness to commit it? Does his Dark

---

[45] Translated from the German "Einheitsübersetzung" of the Bible.

Side reveal itself here (the boar or the dragon?), or is it a simple temptation story, evil enough in itself?

God, according to our understanding today, did not give Abraham a command in an audible voice, making Himself so clearly known that the pious, obedient Abraham could not refuse the command. However, we must keep in mind that for Abraham a refusal of the command would have been very conceivable. We may recall the earlier story in which God tells Abraham of His plan to destroy Sodom and Gomorrah. Abraham accomplishes the unheard of and questions this decision. He reminds God of his responsibility: "Will you really destroy the guilty and the blameless without distinction?... You are the supreme judge of the whole earth, therefore you must not violate the law." Let us also not forget that Isaac was not the only son, just the only truly beloved one. The other one, namely, Ishmael, had been cast out with God's consent. So here again the image of the repressed Dark One.

Anyone who hears voices today is admitted to a psychiatric ward. He is considered to be mentally ill. But even if no voices are heard, no one today would dare to pass off an inner urge to kill his own son as a divine order. In any case, it is quite certain that we would either ascribe such a way of thinking and behaving to the devil, a counter-god, or simply describe it as insane. Hardly anyone would have the courage to make the Dark Side of the One God responsible for it.

When considering the terrible crimes that are committed in many places in the name of God and religion, such a way of thinking is, of course, also highly dangerous. But simply attributing them to the wickedness of man and/or Satan as an anti-God does not solve the problem, but rather exacerbates it. In any case, the dualistic fundamentalists and fanatics perpetrate all these atrocities, while the decisive act in fact did not occur in the case of Abraham. Some label the dark as demonic and project it outward onto some scapegoat they have so determined, which they then fight. The others, Abraham and his spiritual children, recognize the Dark as something primordial and as something mysteriously and terribly divine, but do not fall prey to it in the end. Rather, the dark is transformed by an equally mysterious process in which suffering from the conflict between reality and the goal of desire makes man not only the crucible of conflict, but also the place where the love of the transcendent God finally overflows everything and makes liberation, the spiritual progress of man and the indwelling God, possible.

The divine elemental force is both a restraining, aggravating one and a pushing, driving one, like a bow with a mounted arrow is stretched further and further until the collected tensioning force is sufficient to drive the arrow to its target. Only then is the arrow released. In our image, man is both bow and arrow. The divine elemental force tensions the bow, thus seemingly pulling in the wrong direction at first, but then releases the arrow at the right moment, which then flies in the "right" direction.

One's own breast, one's own heart, one's own soul is therefore the place of conflict, of the attempt for integration, of the coexistence of opposites and finally also of the miracle. The decisive thing here is that there is hope that the inner conflict will not be carried destructively, instead of salutarily, and neither inwardly nor outwardly, as a violent conflict.

For our purposes today, this probably means that Abraham was plagued by various thoughts that he could not let go of. The survivors of the story boldly put God himself as their source, a courageous step that should give us food for thought.

Two thoughts emerge as a possibility:

On the one hand, Abraham must have asked himself whether it was also his duty to sacrifice his firstborn, as was apparently customary in that region at the time. Even if this meant that the promise of descendants and thus the expectation of the continuation of his path would be called into question. With such thoughts, he dealt with the common custom, a custom that was, however, more than what we imagine it to be nowadays, namely something that was connected with an inner compulsion, a compulsion that everyone had to submit to without much thought, no matter how great the sacrifice.

Is such compulsion a manifestation of the dark indwelling God?

This question is clearly and positively explained in the traditions which have been handed down to us. This inner compulsion is equated with the voice of God.

The other line of thought is closer to our understanding, but at the same time related to the first. It is about the old sacrificing the young in order to survive themselves. This can be observed even to this day in every military conflict. The (young) soldiers are sent to war and to death by the (older) generals and politicians, ultimately in order to sacrifice themselves for them—on the surface, in order to protect them from their enemies. While behind the scenes and probably also in terms of depth psychology, in order to give life to the others through their death, or more precisely, a continuation of life that suppresses their fear of dying—at least for a short time. This is an image and a sentiment that also resonates in common Christian ideas about the meaning of Jesus' death on the cross.

Since the sacrifice of the firstborn also ultimately served to appease the deity and thus to save the elders (similar to the dragon stories), both thoughts have the same root, namely a selfish one: appeasing God to save one's own life. This is how the story presents itself from man's point of view.

From God's point of view (of course, ultimately from the point of view of the human observer), God instigates man to sacrifice his son in order to appease or reconcile God, that is, himself. This is what the Greek Bible says, in which the same story is repeated grandly and exaggeratedly with the accounts of Jesus' life and death, albeit with a different outcome. While in the Hebrew Bible the human sacrifice is not performed, according to the Greek Bible Jesus goes the way of sacrifice to the bitter end on the cross.

Martin Buber says that the story of the unperformed sacrifice of Isaac documents for Judaism the final renunciation of human sacrifice. The consciousness of man in common Christianity has not yet developed that far. In any case, for most Christians, the idea of sacrifice still plays a central role in the conception of the meaning of Jesus' crucifixion.

Returning to our story and our speculation about the deliberations of Abraham that brought him to the point of setting out with his son for his sacrifice, despite his earlier demonstrated skepticism concerning God's will.

He acted under inner compulsion, overwhelmed by the thought that the sacrifice was God's will and was inevitable. It must have been a journey through hell: three days on the road, without giving his companions any closer explanation, ultimately alone with himself, his questions and doubts and his inner torment. Then, at the altar of sacrifice, the horrible moment of truth, when Isaac finally understood that he himself was to be the sacrifice and thereupon looking into his father's eyes. This shattering moment probably triggered the turning point. The strength to do so probably came from the all-overpowering divine love—the love of Abraham for his son, the love of life par excellence, which became stronger than the willingness to kill.

The Hebrew Bible does speak of an angel who called a halt. Strangely enough, the message did not come directly from God. Perhaps He was surprised by the unexpected development and resented it, which is why He only sent a messenger. The experience with God in the previous story of the deal between God and Abraham over Sodom and Gomorrah allows for this possibility. The commentators do not seem to rule this out. In any case, it cannot be without significance that, according to the text, God gives the order Himself, thus identifying Himself with it unreservedly, but sends only an angel for the revocation, thus not identifying Himself with it unreservedly. Once more, this man, who is standing out of the general state of consciousness, seems to be more sensitive and merciful than the indwelling God, whose consciousness corresponds to that of the generality. To put this more precisely, this could mean that this man becomes the place where, the higher development of the indwelling God wants and has to occur.

Starting with Rupert Sheldrake, it would probably have to be stated that the morphic field of that time was the common conviction that to appease the deity the firstborn had to be sacrificed. This morphic field is the garment of the indwelling deity, perhaps even his form, in any case the prison of behavioral forms which God has imposed upon himself with the incarnation in his creation. The liberation from this prison can take place only by new morphic fields that gain form in the human breast.

Abraham struggles through to the realization that the cosmic God of infinite love does not want and does not need this sacrifice. This is the "latent possibility" of which Sheldrake speaks. Thus a new morphic field arises, very weak only because conceived by only one person in opposition to a broad majority of others and ultimately realized. The old morphic field, the indwelling God himself, seems to resist, sends itself—figuratively speaking—grudgingly into the change. Therefore it does not speak itself, but merely sends a messenger.

Today, we would probably say that the angel represented the result of Abraham's inner jolting, which called this into question and led to a different conclusion than the one planned. At the decisive moment, the inner compulsion to kill was transformed by the love of life. Abraham did not slaughter his son and never again after him was a ritual human sacrifice performed in Judaism. In Judaism, from then on, man was sure that God did not want it and had no need of it. Most Christians do not believe this until this very day! Expressing it the other way round: The God indwelling in Judaism was brought forward by this story by an essential step on the way to the unification with his cosmic side of infinite love, that is, the latent possibility. Therefore, it is not surprising that

Abraham has become the symbol of grace, compassion and love for Judaism.

Probably the custom of the North American Indians before the wars against the whites, not to kill the enemy in conflicts with other tribes, but to land a coup or to cut off his scalp, is due to something similar to the Abraham experience. Perhaps a similar ritual also applied to the European knights. Regrettably, all this has been buried by the introduction of far-reaching weapons, up to and including the "modern" weapons of mass destruction. The shattering experience of the face-to-face encounter has thus been excluded, and with it the possibility of an inner change of heart triggered by it and a conversion. Long-range weapons, as this story shows, rather represent an escape reaction, by which such an encounter is to be consciously or unconsciously prevented. The fact that thereby the human being is not only blocked in his spiritual development, but even mentally crippled, remains unnoticed, although this would be of extraordinary importance for all of us. In this respect the use of long-range weapons is to be compared to the Siegfried reaction.

Encouragingly, although unfortunately, only once and of limited duration, a nation once managed to abolish the already introduced firearms, because their use was incompatible with the dignity, the nature and the way of man. Surprisingly, it was the Japanese who did so. After the Portuguese had introduced firearms they were used there for a long time. The technical prerequisites were there and foundry and forging were already highly developed at that time. Nevertheless, firearms were eventually reduced to ritual use in much the same way that the Chinese knew and used gunpowder but not for warfare for centuries. Unfortunately, the opening of Japan to the West in the nineteenth century led to a return to Western technology and thinking, which—as we all know—led straight to an outbreak of colonialism and imperialism, first in military, and today mainly in economic form, in the "best" Western way of thinking.

What is to be learned from this for our daily lives and especially for our dealings with the Dark Side of God, with the boar or the dragon?

It seems to me to be decisive that Abraham first followed his inner compulsion and descended into his inner hell. If I remember correctly, this is called the "paradoxical intervention" in modern psychology. He embarks on a path that, on the face of it, leads to his own destruction. But it is only this path that leads to the decisive scene of truth, the change with respect to the recognition between father and son; a change of view that was not only horrible but also healing, whatever psychological damage and scarring it may have left on father and son. Both of them will not have had any illusions about God and man afterwards, although once again it had worked out favorably. There was no room for one-sided ideas about the " loving" father and the "loving" God after this terrible experience; the horror had come too close to them for that. But the horror is embraced, integrated and transformed as a possibility for man, as his own possibility, and therefore as a possibility for God. The history of the ritual human sacrifice is brought to an end in Judaism, unfortunately not for mankind in general, as not only the witch burnings, the Holocaust, the black masses and our traffic victims prove every day. So the path is not over yet, even if the necessary steps are clear for everyone to see.

Perhaps the ultimate point of the path will never be reached. Such final point would be the hour of the cosmic Messiah. Leibowitz, in his manner of looking at things, probably was right in saying, "The Messiah who has come is not the Messiah."[46] For Gandhi, however, the way was the goal. In this sense, Jesus is the Messiah,

---

46 Leibowitz, Gespräche über Gott und die Welt, Frankfurt 1990.

for he not only showed the way; he himself walked it. This means that it is about a "coexistence of opposites", as the Far East teaches, but it should be a dynamic and not a static coexistence, which aims at a change of man and of the indwelling God. To stay with the story of Abraham: it is about a development which wants to achieve in man that he no longer believes that he or God needs the sacrifice of other men, at the same time freeing the indwelling God from this prison.

The desired change, however, must not fall prey to the mania of feasibility. After all, it is not only about a change of man and of the indwelling God, but precisely because it is about both, about a change with the help of divine energies and probably also according to a divine "time schedule" in the sense of a realization of latent possibilities, as this is also demonstrated by the Jesuanic image of the grain of wheat as a seed. It is about a peculiar connection of "wanting by not wanting", as it is called by Lao Tse, thus about an energetic support of growth and maturing processes, which are to be guessed rather intuitively than to be pushed forward energetically by planning. In any case, at least as much happens with us as wants and should happen through us. It is therefore probably more about a "laisser-être" than about a "laisser-faire". The ideal behavior would be achieved if we, metaphorically speaking, reach for a ripe apple exactly when it wants to detach itself from the tree and not before, because then it would not yet be fully ripe, and also not later, because then it would already lie on the ground as fallen fruit.

After all this it seems to need two things: on the one hand the initial readiness to submit to the existing morphic fields, thus also according to own character and behavior patterns. That would correspond to the order of God and the readiness of Abraham to the sacrifice. On the other hand the formation of new morphic fields, through which latent possibilities are realized. This would correspond to the angel's objection and Abraham's insight that the time of the ritual human sacrifice was over and that it is necessary to act accordingly. But the way to the goal leads over the recognition of existing reality as a reality of the human being and the indwelling God.

Thus, both are needed. On the one hand, obedience to the former order—that is what the institutionalized churches, as successors of the established priesthood, make their main task. On the other hand, however, there is also the constant struggle for the realization of latent possibilities, i.e. the inner potential—this is the prophetic task of the question of God's will and the search for divine visions for earthly reality. It is equally important. Without the challenge of the search for renewal, the one tends to solidify in outdated forms and norms of behavior, and thus to stagnation and death. The other is threatened by the wild growth of sectarianism.

It only remains to try to explain what the wild boar, the dragon and the story of Abraham and Isaac have to do with each other. The connection of these three pictorial stories is logically difficult to justify. It forced itself upon me from within. But I will nevertheless try to give a reason, even if perhaps a flimsy one.

From my point of view, it is a question of dealing with the Dark Side of Man and God in all three cases, of the path of liberation of Man and God, which presupposes the "dynamic co-existence of opposites". Ultimately, then, for me it is the same whether we are dealing with the inner boar, the inner dragon, or our willingness to sacrifice our real future, "the Son", to the indwelling God for the sake of our own illusory future. It is always a matter of learning to deal with it in the right way.

But what does that mean—to deal with it in the right way?

The Nativity

I cannot do much with the way the birth of Jesus is celebrated in churches today, and I know many people, especially younger ones, who seem to feel the same way. I will therefore try to find out what Christmas means to me concretely as the starting point of Christianity, even if the result of this search is nothing more than something subjective and individual that is not necessarily essential to others, except as an impulse to clarify for oneself what of that which has come down to us could become "salutary"[47] as individual truth.

First of all, it is important to know that—as already stated elsewhere1—the feast day of the birth of Jesus was moved to December 25. Originally, it was the Feast of the Apparitions, the day that is still celebrated today in the Eastern Church as Jesus' birthday. By moving it to December 25, the image of Jesus was united with the idea of the Roman sun god Sol Invictus, the invincible one, whose holiday falls at the time as the winter solstice. This symbolically highly significant step sealed the transformation

[47] cf. "Die heilsame Alternative", Wuppertal 1989.

of the Jewish Messiah, epitome of the suffering, serving servant of God, into the Greco-Roman Christ.

The one ended ignominiously on the cross and ranks among the failed even to this day as the history of Christianity also illustrates—even though he did not remain among the dead. The other is a victorious type, of whom it is said in a chorale: "Jesus Christ reigns as King..."

One is something like an antagonist of Caesar or, better, "the salutary alternative" who exposes "the Roman power devilry" (Carl Gustav Jung); the other not only takes over the Caesars' insignia, he becomes their successor, stamping the history of the Church through the centuries with the Caesarian stamp, both in its historical impact and in its dogmatic doctrinal edifice.

One brings the seedlings of more feminine traditions, such as non-violence and renunciation of power, back to flower; the other becomes the iron pillar of patriarchal structures of rule, for whom the Crusades and other religious wars, as well as witch burnings and the extermination of inconvenient minorities, are no more than "the continuation of politics by other means".

One recognizes that God "lets the sun shine on the good and the wicked" and recommends "going the second mile" in dealing with coercion and violence, i.e. the powerfully conscious, not weakly unconscious yielding, which seeks dialogue and does not aim at immediate success and result, but lets the other (and the Dark One) go its own inner way of change calmly and with understanding, often painfully experiencing that the necessary change takes longer than hoped. The other is dualistic and thinks "here good, there evil". The vindication of "just" wars is therefore not difficult for him. He overlooks the fact that so-called evil is not only outside but also inside and that, according to Martin Buber, "the Archimedean point for the change of the world is the change of oneself."

I realize that I do not want to have anything to do with a Christmas as a celebration of the birth of the Christ, the Greek-Roman sun-god in Jewish-messianic guise, no matter how widespread this idea may be. Surely, however, it has to be recognized as an aberration.

Maybe we can extract that out of it.

Let us begin with the central Christian claim, the incarnation of God in Jesus.

God is born as a man in the deepest darkness, namely the long night of winter. Not in the darkness of Satan, the counter-god, but in the darkness that is as much God's as the light.

This darkness may embody the Satanic, but Satan, according to the Hebrew Bible, is one of the sons of God, that is, the Dark Side of the Divine Being. The Hebrew Bible and with it Judaism know only one God and not a light, good one and a dark, evil one, namely the devil, like common Christianity. Already their most important mnemonic sentence "Hear, Israel, HE our God, HE is one" makes this clear. According to this, there is only one God, to whom everything that we believe to experience in the divine (or also counter-divine) must be attributed. Their monotheism is consistent up to the frightening insight that God also has a Dark Side according to our perception. As Carl Gustav Jung makes clear in his book "Answer to Job," man's realization of the Dark Side of God leads first to great inner disquiet, but then to the realization that God has become man, that God is not only the perpetrator but also the victim of our fate. This fate is therefore not only imposed on us by God; He bears it with us. He suffers from it together with us.

Both insights belong together. In this respect, the incarnation of God and thus also the Christmas feast is, if not completely meaningless, without the experience of His Dark Side, then it is without terrible and fruitful tension.

Whether both aspects, the insight that God is a perpetrator and the insight that God also becomes a victim through his incarnation, can be established historically is for many an open question. According to the Hebrew Bible, the first point is made repeatedly in Jewish history. In the book of Job, it is consistently taken to its logical conclusion, and the depth of the human misery revealed by it breaks open unsparingly: Man is authored by God, he is his plaything. For the Christian, the answer to this comes with the historically definable birth of Jesus, with which the incarnation of God takes place.

Unfortunately, this story was overloaded with many non-Jewish ideas. While this promoted its dissemination in the Greco-Roman cultural area, it has essentially excluded the pious, monotheistic Jew to this day.

The image of the incarnated God appears for the devout Jew, as far as I know, only with the Kabbalah, even if the roots of it go back to pre-Christian times. The indwelling God, the female Shechina, is spoken of only from the Middle Ages on, but her relationship with the pre-Christian Sophia, Wisdom, and the Ruach, the Holy Spirit, is unmistakable.

The Shechina accompanies the human being into the exile of this side of the world. As described in detail, Elie Wiesel reports from the concentration camp where he has to witness how a hanged boy is unable to die. When he asks where God actually is in this terrible situation, he learns within himself that God is in there hanging on the gallows.

In the Judeo-Christian tradition, the human consciousness that sees in God both the perpetrator and the victim of human fate has been evident for about a thousand years at the very latest. Jews and Christians can lament and denounce their strokes of fate at first, like Job, and then accept them more easily with the consoling insight that they are not alone in their misery, but that God is suffering with them. Not as a light in the darkness, in which God is the light and man the darkness, but that God—to stay with this image—is also the darkness, as it says in a Psalm: "And if I lay me down in hell, behold, Thou art also there." As an integrating "component".

Furthermore, it is important to know that the place of the Incarnation is not the world of the elite, but of the marginalized, the poor and homeless, that is, the darker end of the social scale. The Incarnation of God, or His indwelling, is for everyone, even primarily for the Dark Ones. There is no mistaking this, even if Christianity today is primarily a religion of the upper middle class, in Christian countries themselves and mostly even in the rest of the world.

Then there is another point that concerns me, which, for those bound to the Christian tradition, calls into question the whole story of God's incarnation: the virgin birth.

For those who believe in the virgin birth, Jesus is at least a demigod, begotten of God, born of a man. This means that the Incarnation is only fragmentary, at most half complete. It is only complete when the Father too is undisputedly a man. Yes, if no one is to be excluded because of an inferior social status, then this would mean that Jesus must have been an illegitimate child and his mother anything but an "immaculate virgin".

It is evident from the fact that with great effort an ancestral line is presented for Jesus (by the way not even a uniform one), which would only make sense if he was not begotten by God or the Holy Spirit, but had a father whose name is at the end of this line. That this was already a point of contention in the time of the Gospels is evident from the fact that with great effort an ancestral line is presented for Jesus (by the way not even a uniform one), which would only make sense if he was not begotten by God or the Holy Spirit, but had a father whose name is at the end of this line.

Since this question has not yet been clearly worked out and answered in Christianity, it means that the incarnation of God in man par excellence, i.e. in each one of us, has not yet been accepted and accomplished in the general consciousness of Christianity. Nor, therefore, has the direct experience of God in each one and, consequently, the direct access of each individual to God. It is true that in the already quoted Christmas carol by Angelus Silesius it says: "If Christ were born a thousand times in Bethlehem and not in you, you would still be lost." This, however, is still not the general insight and consciousness today.

Until now, it seems that we have simply not dared to follow through with the idea of the Incarnation, of God's humanity within us, to the point where we are really able to perceive and accept it with body and soul, as the innermost part of our own person. Judging from Christian history, this is extraordinarily difficult. Jesus, Mary and also the saints are still considered mediators for our relationship with God and indispensable for us. As the old prayer "Holy Mary, pray for us poor sinners..." shows, this is probably primarily related to our sinner consciousness and our lack of conception of the Dark Side of God because, for mainstream Christianity, God is good and man is evil.

The Mohammedans, the Muslims, seem to have taken a further step of spiritual development on this point. Their founder of religion, Mohammed, is unreservedly regarded as a human being, as a prophet. He is also no stranger to sin.

With the conception of God as the perpetrator and victim of human destiny, at the end of the development of consciousness, there is communion of man with God, indissoluble unity, there is the divine man, for the Christian the man who resembles Jesus. This is man on the way of the union of the divine forces from above and from below, which make his life fearful and fruitful at the same time in a great arc of tension.

This reveals the second essential of the Christmas story: the birth of the new man.

The Christian conception of Jesus, as far as it opens itself to the Jewish-Messianic images, sees the "first new man" from the Jewish tradition, as Franz Alt calls Jesus in his book of the same name, namely a man who represents the characteristics described at the beginning and thus a salutary alternative to the Caesarian ideal image and is characterized by warm-hearted benevolence for all living things. Whether all this really happened historically, we shall never know. But the evangelists describe Jesus in this way, and his image shines through the centuries in a way that could not be obscured by all the distortions and trivializations. It gives his humanity a divine quality, and it does so from an archetypal depth for which historical details ultimately become secondary.

With the birth and life of Jesus, however, the process of God's incarnation has not been completed. On the one hand, it is continued in every human being, making Jesus "the first among the sons of men". This is difficult enough to accept, because it devalues much of Christian doctrine or even declares it false (such as his mediatorial role described above). But the second is even more problematic. Our image of Jesus represents only the Light Side, the (superficially) Good Side of God. The Dark Side of God breaks out in the temptation story immediately before the beginning of Jesus' public ministry. However, this is not the only place where it is mentioned. Furthermore, it has been handed down that this was not accepted and "integrated" by Jesus, but rejected and rejected. Indeed, it is said, "Depart from me, get thee away, away with thee, Satan." This is a phrase that, regardless of what may have really happened, has always triggered and justified the struggle, oppression, secession and repression in Christianity. This story of temptation, then, has an entirely different inflection than the comparable story in Abraham.

All this suggests that so far in Christianity the incarnation of the Dark Side of God in Jesus has not been conceivable and acceptable. Christian consciousness has so far neither seen nor admitted this necessity. The only approach to this can be seen in the fact that—albeit unconsciously—Christ was factually equated with the Roman sun god Sol Invictus. In any case, in the gospels the Dark Side of God is omitted.

It is only the Book of Revelation that is aware of this. The reports of the gospels about Satan, according to the Hebrew Bible one of the sons of God, but with the Christians a counter-god, and about Judas, a kind of counterpart of Jesus on the human level, are too sketchy, faint and without archetypal power to really fill this role.

The consequence of this absence or unconsciousness concerning the divine Darkness is that this incarnation must still take place if we no longer want to remain helplessly, because unconsciously, at the mercy of the Dark.

The image of the beast actually does appear in the Book of Revelation[48]. For example, it says there:

"And I saw a beast coming out of the sea..."

---

[48] Chapters 13 and 14.

This means that the dark reality of the "beast" rises from the sea of the unconscious, thus becoming conscious to us. That it is a "part" of God, however, is concealed and probably not conveyed (at least I have never heard it so). Similar is the case with the other verse:

"If anyone worships the beast and his image.... he shall drink of the wine of the wrath of God."

Here, too, it is correctly stated that the "beast" is not to be worshipped, that is, not to be worshipped without question. The text conceals, however, and thus abets the Christian dualism, that it cannot be eliminated by fighting.

We have to face, metaphorically speaking, the inner darkness, the inner dragon, also the beast of Revelation, but not to try to fight it down and destroy it, but to "integrate" it, to love it and thus to open the way to its redemption, to its liberation. The fairy tales say that for every head cut off by a dragon, one or even more grow back. So the ancients already knew that he could not be overcome in this way. And yet we still hold on to this idea today. The biblical images of the dragon[49] also cultivate this way of thinking for our understanding.

---

49 For example, Revelation 12 ff.

The Nativity

William Butler Yeats seems to have felt the dualistic aberration of the Christianized white man and the resulting challenge in an almost visionary way when he wrote:

... somewhere in sands of the desert
A shape with lion body and the head of a man,
A gaze blank and pitiless as the sun,
Is moving its slow thighs, while all about it
Reel shadows of the indignant desert birds.
The darkness drops again; but now I know
That twenty centuries of stony sleep
Were vexed to nightmare by a rocking cradle,
And what rough beast, its hour come round at last,
Slouches towards Bethlehem to be born?[50]

Who would deny that the Dark is a raw beast for us and that we are addicted to it, that therefore there is a need for a new or yet a newly understood Christmas? The prerequisite for this seems to be that this beast is born into our consciousness as the Dark Side of God. Then we can begin to go our way, which is comparable to the way of Abraham and the way of Jesus.

To realize this, we should learn to make two essential changes in the Lord's Prayer. Perhaps

---

50 From: "The Second Coming", a poem written by Irish poet W. B. Yeats in 1919.

then we will become open to what is at stake today:

Lead us into temptation
and free us also from all darkness.

The Unification of Opposites

When I had to go to the hospital last year because of a heart condition, an image appeared in my mind's eye that reminded me of a vision as described in Ezekiel in the 37th chapter:

A gray, empty plain covered by thin fog in gloomy twilight, illuminated only by a streak of light on the horizon, of which I did not know at first whether this was the evening or the dawn. My gaze seemed to go in a northwesterly direction, and I felt as if I were looking at a summer night, a time when dusk and dawn merge. Essentially, however, there was a gray, gloomy mood that did not let me go for months.

Later, I reread the story, and the differences between the two images became clear to me. In Ezekiel, God asked the prophet about the plain covered with dead men's bones:

"Son of man, will these bones live?"...
"I said, my Lord,
YOU, you yourself know.

> *And he said to me:*
> *Proclaim over these bones,*
> *say to them:*
> *you withered bones,*
> *hear HIS words!*
> *Thus asked my Lord, HE, spoken to these bones:*
> *There, I cause the Spirit to blow in you, and you shall live."...*
> *And so it happened.*

There was no voice in my image. There was only the dead, gray, gloomy plain.

The scene depicts a hopeless situation, a dead end from which there is no way out, the end of hope for spiritual progress, for the history of salvation altogether.

This picture seems to me to reflect our situation and also concretely the situation of mainstream psychology in view of the fact that—as Jung describes it—evil has become the determining reality in our time[51]. It is true that it correctly takes the first and probably decisive step, namely the affirmation of reality. But then it does not know how to proceed. Dietmar Pieper writes, referring to violence as an expression of evil[52]:

---

51 cf. page 22
52 Spiegel essay 7/94

"What we need is not the illusion of nonviolence, but an education in violence that does not deny evil, but rather practices dealing with it."

He ends his series of thoughts as follows: "Saying goodbye to self-delusions is particularly painful if no new illusion takes their place. Civil courage and the principle of responsibility, which are urged for many good reasons, are unfortunately no good surrogates. That is why we are currently experiencing not so much an increase in violence in society, as a dismantling without replacement of illusions of the Christian occidental communist kind. Violence, always practiced and always rejected, is perceived particularly ruthlessly. Until a new illusion mercifully covers our split in consciousness again."

Honest, unsparing, but ultimately hopeless—this is the only way to comment on it.

Even if it seems difficult, almost impossible: The right starting point is quite obviously first the willingness and then the ability to perceive evil, violence or, in Jewish tradition religiously expressed, the Dark Side of the One God. For those who are shaped by Christian religion, everything resists this. Perhaps a dream image, reported by Veronica Gradl, will help us further[53]:

"The woman is walking along the edge of a country road through spring-like countryside. Further ahead is a village. On the other side of the road, someone is coming towards her. Arriving at the same point, he turns fully toward her, looking at her. His silent, worn face sketches that he is an unhoused, a living and an unprotected person, strong in his vulnerability; a vagrant, a world-changer, a fighter and a lover—Christ and Satan in one person—'the Messiah'.

From his bright eyes, his gaze meets her in awesome recognition.

She knows with trepidation that the decision lies with her alone: will she close herself off in sudden fright before this unknown stranger? Will she greet him fleetingly and pass by?

Or will she answer his gaze? Will she turn to him as he did to her?

What will he say to her?"

Before the challenge to answer these questions, to answer correctly, is the courage to recognize in the dream figure "Christ and Satan in one person—the Messiah". For a proper Christian this is blasphemous. However, we will not be able to avoid it.

---

[53] Veronika Gradl, Die Ruhe des siebten Tages und die Ohnmacht der Kraft, Innsbruck 1988 (?).

This painful realization goes a significant step further than the following story by Erwin Reisner[54]:

"It is the time of the solar eclipse that precedes the earthquake. Through the night, like phosphorus, the pale body shines, but it shines without illuminating. Even the stars have lost their light; for all brightness HE has taken into Himself.

Loneliness surrounds the cross, and the earth is as if extinct. Then, between death rattles, the Savior cries out across the wasteland: 'God, my God! Why have you forsaken me!' His call finds no echo. Nature no longer recognizes the voice, as it no longer knows the Light. But out of the Darkness, the Counter-God comes forth. Enthroned on black clouds, he floats closer to the cross. It is Shiva, the destroyer, it is Priapos with the obscene symbol, with the mocking grimace of what is called love. And the idol speaks:

'Whom do you call? Only we are still there; only you and I, your eternal opposition, nothing else. You call for the God whom you have taken upon yourself. In your striving for your own divinity you have de-godified the world. Where is there still a God besides you?

---

54 Quoted from Samuel Widmer, Ins Herz der Dinge lauschen, Solothurn 1989.

You wanted to eradicate your hatred, but by raising your sword against it, you fell to it. Now your creature has turned against you and nailed you to the cross. See, I am your creature, the spawn of your own hatred. You wanted to destroy me, but you have fattened me.

When I promised you the treasures of the world at that time, if you fell down before me, you spurned them, you already hated the works of Him, whom you now call, because you wanted to be like Him; then you scornfully replied: It is written: You shall worship the Lord your God and be subject to Him alone.

Where is your master now, if not me; for nothing is left but the two of us. I, too, must perish at the moment you die. But was that all of your proud life's work? Thou didst teach: Love your enemies! Now love me, your worst and last enemy.

Only because your love was not perfect did you create me as you see me in my hideous distortion before you. At that time in the desert I was beautiful. Once again I command you now to adore me. Love me! Know that I am your God, your Father.'

Then Jesus slowly raises his head and his eyes are fixed on the terrible face of the enemy. Then, transfigured by boundless love, he says to him: 'Father, into your hands I commend my spirit!'

And the light that emanates from the holy body begins to illuminate the earth again. The sun emerges, and the black clouds, the throne of the counter-god, dissolve into nothing."

The devil in Reisner's story is the counter-god who corresponds to the dualistic Christian image of "here good, there evil". In the first image, the Messiah is both Satan and Christ at the same time. This is the true man. That is I.

The temptation of dualistic separation is very great in Reisner's way of looking at things. It is overcome, however, by the loving devotion described.

Perhaps it is necessary to really imagine the Dark as a counterpart in order to be able to "deal" with it. Perhaps the perception presupposes the confrontation in the actual literal sense. Finally, however, we must realize that the Dark is indeed something of its own and not something that is alien, that it is something divine and not something satanic that coming from a counter-god.

So it may be helpful at first to see the Dark Side of God as a counterpart in order to be able to perceive it at all, in the way Samuel Widmer describes it in the aforementioned book:

"I experienced something similar (as in dealing with the figure of Judas—author's note) in dealing with the evil par excellence, the devil. My therapist at that time also had to serve for a God-transference, so that I could lovingly integrate the devil as the other part of God's unity in me again."

On the subject of his account, he writes decisive sentences for our further development in dealing with the Dark:

"... that your feelings towards others are always, and I really mean always, transmissions, projections from the past and from the part of your being that you have not yet integrated. Little by little you will realize that the only way to meet others that will allow you and them to live without conflict has to come directly from your very core, from your heart. That is, basically, to meet without expectations, without emotional attitude, without role, always new and direct."

This is a long journey, however. Nevertheless, one thing is certain: "Only reconciliation with these feelings can open the door to love."[55]

The crucial thing seems to be that we first of all give space to the Dark within us. It is there anyway, but it is necessary to consciously af-

---

55 ibid.

firm it as part of our self. Psychology also goes thus far. Now begins the mysterious. Veronica Gradl writes about this[56]:

"What the intellect and all the loftiest thoughts cannot do, the impotent, vulnerable most secret desire of the ego can do."

The desire to give love and maintain relationship nudges any drive into the center of the whole person in such a way that a concentric ordering of body, soul and intellect becomes possible.

Under the dominion of this desire (which seems so obsolete, so unattainable, so unrealistic and naive), a person can begin to persistently and patiently ask the question:

How does my longing fit with what I think? How does my idea of what I want to be like as a human being fit with the forces I feel within me? How does my need fit with the desires of the other person? How does all this fit into the fine and strict grid of love (which does not reject, does not condemn, does not kill, does not divide, does not use violence, and does not hate)?

By thus asking and not desisting, he will have the amazing experience of being transformed, in a wholly unpredictable way, ... then,

---

56 In the quoted book.

in a slow and laborious process of growth, with pain and effort, his being will be recreated ..."

This is the incarnation of latent potentiality, of the infinite love of the transcendent God.

On the one hand, we experience the divine elemental force as the Dark within us, as the Indwelling, as the Emanating, as Franz Werfel calls it. But that is not all. The transcendent God of infinite love, the Emanating, to stay with Franz Werfel, also desires to be born in us, to take shape, but not as something emanated and firmly outlined, but as a latent potential, not as something compelling, but as something becoming, vulnerable, uninhabited, as the "child in us": the child in us, sensitive and susceptible, in need of warmth and love. This is probably what Angelus Silesius sensed when he wrote: "If Christ had been born a thousand times in Bethlehem and not in you..." For in our image of the child of Bethlehem "lying woeful, naked and bare in a manger," as a Christmas carol says, the basic archetypal truth outlined becomes a reality for Christianity. The Christmas celebrations bear witness to it, even if they usually reflect no more than a dull foreboding and we only slowly begin to grasp this reality in its comprehensive significance.

It is true that modern psychology also knows about the "child in us", but unfortunately it does not know that this is also the latent potentiality of the transcendent God Who wants to gain space in us, for Whom we are to "prepare a place". We should learn to perceive the polarity of both sides in us, the bringing forth, the being, which manifests itself mostly as the Dark, and the bringing forth, the becoming, but also the longing, the tension of love between both poles that urges their union. If we then begin to prepare a place for both within ourselves through the way we deal with one another, then, as a latent potential, the Divine Darkness within us can give birth to the Divine Light within us through the Divine Love present in us, then the wholesome path can begin, then it is Christmas.

www.ingramcontent.com/pod-product-compliance
Lightning Source LLC
LaVergne TN
LVHW032202070526
838202LV00007B/278